Anonymous

The Christian's Wedding Ring

Anonymous

The Christian's Wedding Ring

ISBN/EAN: 9783337719890

Printed in Europe, USA, Canada, Australia, Japan

Cover: Foto ©Lupo / pixelio.de

More available books at **www.hansebooks.com**

MOST REVD FRANCIS FULFORD D.D.

THE CHRISTIAN'S WEDDING RING,

CONTAINING

FIVE LETTERS,

AND A

SERIES OF POEMS,

WRITTEN BY A LADY

WITH THE SINCERE DESIRE OF SOWING THE SEEDS OF UNION
IN THE CHRISTIAN CHURCH.

Dedicated
TO THE MEMORY OF A BELOVED MOTHER.

Montreal:
PRINTED BY THE LOVELL PRINTING AND PUBLISHING CO.
ST. NICHOLAS STREET.
1874.

INTRODUCTION.

"WHAT IS TRUTH?"

Our God abundant is in Truth,
Love and practise it in youth,
It is the only outward sign
Of an inward grace Divine.

Let nations altogether plead
For one Holy Truthful creed;
One that will Christ-like fruits produce,
With a new and fragrant juice.

We will not then to evil cleave,
Nor ourselves and friends deceive;
All will be open, pure and bright,
Each a burning shining light.

While strangers to this wond'rous grace
Doom'd must be the human race;
But when we reproduce this gem,
It the flood of sin will stem.

Search then, for Truth, our God's great gift,
It will all our actions sift;
When we its banner do display
Never more will we decay.

Then all earth's great and mighty throng,
With one universal song
Will chant the Great Creator's praise
As they walk in wisdom's ways.

The Christians' Wedding Ring.

THE SABBATH MORN.

In the quiet of your chamber,
   In the early Sabbath dawn,
Rise and converse with your Maker,
   Like singing-birds in the morn.

We need not now, like Sainted Mary,
   In the grave-clothes seek our Lord,—
You will find Him bright and early,
   He will answer you each word.

From His mansion up above us
   He considers all our ways;
He requires no such work and fuss,
   As man's making now-a-days,

About rituals and crosses,
   And some other foolish things;
'Tis His sacraments he watches,
   To His Sabbath Day he clings.

Oh! watch then, ye men and maidens,
   Try your actions in the light,
God is coming to His garden,
   To make all things pure and bright.

INTRODUCTION TO THE CHRISTIAN'S WEDDING RING.

O let me sing a note of praise,
   Let ev'ry note through earth resound,
One that will make all voices raise
   A strain to draw all nations round.

It must be simple, sweet and pure,
   Each heart must play upon the string,
The harmonies must be so sure
   That earth will loud its praises ring.

Five tones this melody requires,
   Four parts to be together sung,
A skilful leader full of fire,
   With instruments in concert strung.

The words all drawn from Holy Writ,
   That source from which all knowledge springs,
Without the hollow earthly wit
   Which constantly around us rings.

Hear! oh ye kings, give ear princess!
   Christian unity I sing.
Let our love, the heart's best incense,
   All heathen minds to Jesus bring.

When we weed and rake our garden,
   Cherish this sweet and lovely plant,—
Earth will be the lovely Eden
   All our senses will enchant.

The curse Christ will from earth efface
   When we in love God's truth embrace;
Man's labor will some work achieve—
   The Tree of Life will drop its seed.

To Her Royal Highness Victoria Adelaide Mary Louisa, Crown Princess of Prussia.

DEAR CHRISTIAN PRINCESS:

You who have tasted all the happiness that is to be found in the world in its present state, and have also in the death of your dear father been made perfect through suffering, will perhaps be prepared to look forward with one of the humble subjects of Queen Victoria to the time when the evil spirit will be banished from the earth, and man will be restored to that state of perfect happiness in which he was first created; but, before that time can arrive, woman must put forth her energies for the reformation of the world. It was woman's influence that induced man to disobey, it must be woman's influence that will make man obedient. God made light and goodness; man chooses darkness and evil. This world has been and still is the battle-field of two great Spirits; and, from the creation of man, the Evil Spirit has always succeeded in making woman a willing instrument for the accomplishment of his designs; he has had power to tempt her with the pleasures and vanities of the world, but it must not be so now. When the seventh angel sounded we are told "The four and twenty elders which sat before God on their seats fell upon their faces and worshipped God, saying, we give thee thanks, O Lord God Almighty, which art, and wast, and art to come, because thou hast taken to thee thy great power and hast reigned," Rev. xi. 16-17. When God's Holy Spirit reigns the temptations of the world will no longer prevail. From the sentence of Adam we learn that God requires perfect obedience. After God had made known his will to Noah, respecting the ark, we are told that he did according to all that God commanded him. Gen. vi. 22. And to Moses God said "what thing soever I command you observe to do it, thou shall not add thereto nor diminish from it.' Deut. xii. 32. Christ taught His disciples that no divided service would satisfy the great Father of mankind." "Ye cannot serve God and Mammon," Matt. vi. 24, are His own words. Thus it is quite plain if we wish the punishment of our sins to be removed; if we desire our last enemy, death, to be destroyed, and sickness, pain and sorrow to be withdrawn from the earth we must give up all our crooked ways, and adhere closely to the rules laid down and the example set by our Blessed Lord and Saviour in God's holy word. Common sense and one's own conscience tell us that the Bible has been written by men, not angels, under the influence of God's Holy Spirit to guide us to the paths of peace and holiness. All Christians accept it as the word of God. It is an inexhaustible mine, which has through the devices of the evil one produced different kinds of ore. But the Tree of Life, like the gold in the mine, is there, and will be found when Christians make a united effort to dig, purify and circulate the pure metal. There is not a man, woman or child living who in sight of a rich mine would not try and extract some ore for the benefit of his perishing body, yet many pious souls are contented to take the Bible secondhand, leaving the soul's nourishment in the hands of the church or sect to which the accident of birth has attached them. They thus lose the privilege of having direct intercourse with their Maker; they fail to make themselves known to God, and must be in danger of hearing Christ say " verily I say unto you I know you not.—" Matt. xxv. 12. Every individual should search the Scriptures, day by day, for the purpose of learning how to please God, which alone can make us happy; Christ's commandment is "Search the Scriptures.—John v. 39. The disciples searched them daily.—Acts xvii. 11, we learn in them that "God is Love," 1st John iv. 8, and he requires pure love from his creatures. When Christians are united in their mode of worship, they will make love the great principle of their actions, instead of being wrapped up in self and its surroundings. We must bring our minds to see that the whole human race are all children of one great Creator. We will then realize the greatness of the work of creation and redemption, and we will look forward with faith to the time when God will glorify the earth, yes, drive from it evil and its consequences, of sickness, sorrow and death, for could we but give up the little taste of sin that our Father Adam gave us a relish for, this world would become the Paradise it was before the Fall. The first sacred ordinance we are informed of is matrimony; it is true, it is not necessary to salvation, but, if engaged in with the basis of true love and with the blessing of God, it is a sacrament, from the abuse of which springs all the misery in the world. Woman was created to be the comforter, companion, friend of man. When two persons approach the altar with true love in their hearts, imploring God's blessing on their union, breaking a wine glass and spilling the wine, or using a ring as an outward sign, they perform a sacramental service, and Christ's presence at the marriage feast must have been intended to show that it was a sacred service; and by his changing the water into wine, he endeavoured to teach them what he afterwards told them that "they twain shall be one flesh." Death may part, but cannot sever the tie, and though the Devil has induced men to make laws of divorce, no such laws are of any use, for Christ has said "what therefore God hath joined together, let not man put asunder.—" Mat. xix. 6. Now it is engaged in lightly, with little knowledge of each other's character, in fact without anything solid for its basis. The female education is not practical; there is little or no preparation for the solemn service to be engaged in, but the outward adorning of the body. Flirting is the device which the Devil is using to destroy the pure actions of the heart; even little children flirt in this age; the simplicity of childhood is destroyed by it; the habit from practise becomes part of the nature. The married woman must have beaux, one husband is not enough; she in her youth has been deceived, she in turn becomes a deceiver, and life is one constant scene of acting. The holy and sacred feeling of love which God planted in the heart of man, that mystic bond of union, which enables us to anticipate each other's wishes, to live as it were out of self in each other, becoming day by day purer and holier, guiding each other on the road that leads to the Holy City that St. John saw coming down out of Heaven.—Rev. xxi. 2—this love, like the cactus that blooms once in a hundred years, is so seldom seen that when it appears it is not appreciated, and dies out for want of culture. It is the object of the evil spirit to make us believe that happiness consists in outward appearances, to possess riches, honor, and power he persuades us to lie and deceive, slowly fettering on the chains which bind us to the grave. Christian women, to break these chains, destroy the works of the Devil, and arrest the angel of Death, is a noble work; I call you to enlist in it! The English language is the only one that can boast of a word so expressive as the word home; every home should be a haven of rest, a place of happiness, in which the Christian graces should shine as stars in the firmament. When wives and daughters make it the aim of their lives to make home happy, the angel of peace will descend to the earth, bringing with him happiness and plenty. Then wine, which was intended to make glad the heart of man, will no longer prove a mocker and deceiver, but it will strengthen and refresh as God intended it should. Every action of our lives will be guided by principle, and God's glory will be the chief end of man. The members of each household will then try to do some daily duty for the comfort of its inmates; home amusements will be encouraged, and presided over by the parents; and, instead of the constant whirl of excitement which people call pleasure, real happiness will be found in the domestic circle. The majority of mankind will cease to lead a slavish, selfish life in pursuit of gold, for it will appear quite plain that less means are needed to make people truly happy.

The mind and body which now engross all our attention will yield a third of their attentions to the soul. But ere this great Millenium time arrives women have an arduous work to do. There are, you will say, pure and virtuous women called nuns, who have withdrawn from the world; granted, but have not each of these nuns left their home duties unperformed, and could not each nun have done more good in her own home if she had overcome her temptations there than she has done in the convent, for stone walls do not keep men and women from bowing down to Satan's devices. Christ says: "I pray not that thou shouldst take them out of the world, but that thou shouldst keep them from the evil."—John xvii. 15. The evil spirit stirs every heart with envy, jealousy and passion, and makes both religious and irreligious people bow before his idol of gold. No matter where the christian is, one or other of his temptations will overcome him unless his soul, guided by the Holy Spirit, is washed in his Saviour's blood and looks to God alone for strength with which to resist all evil influences. The Blessed Virgin, the mother of Jesus, has set us the example of retiring to our homes in time of trouble, for St. John tells us:

from the hour of our Saviour's crucifixion, "that disciple took her unto his own home."—John xix. 27. If the Blessed Virgin and the disciples could return to their home duties after witnessing such a scene as the crucifixion of our Lord, surely that is the place where we should strive to serve and worship God and learn submission to his will. When Joseph's heart overflows with love for his brother Benjamin, he orders the ruler of the house to "bring these men home, and slay, and make ready."—Genesis xliii. 16. After Samuel anoints Saul to be king, he "sent all the people away, every man to his house."—10th of 1st Sam. 25. Saul also went home to Gibeah.— 26th verse of same. Habakkuk classes " the one who keepeth not at home" with the proud and those who are fond of wine in his 2 chap., v. When Jesus healed the man with the unclean spirit he desired him to "go home to thy friends."— Mark v. 19. Those three beautiful parables in Luke xv. all teach us to rejoice in our homes, first, over any stray sheep which we may help back to the fold; secondly, over any lost jewel, " which may mean virtue," which has been lost and is found, and lastly, over the poor prodigal sinner who returns, after long wandering in the paths of sin, to His Father and his home. There he is to be restored to life. In his home he is to find peace and contentment. See how beautifully Joseph provides, remark, not only for his wife and children, but for his father and brethren in the time of famine. Indeed Genesis seems to provide bread for each household, Genesis xlvii. 12; Exodus a lamb or meat, xii. 3. "According to the house of their fathers a lamb for an house." Leviticus an atonement. The priest is desired in the xvi. chapter to go alone into the tabernacle and make "An atonement for himself and for his househould, and for all the congregation of Israel," 17 verse. Then Numbers teaches us in the xviii. chapter to give a tenth part of our earnings to God. If we do this we may enjoy both the fruit of the vine and the products of the earth, for it is the reward of both ye and your households, Deuteronomy informs us, that God will reward us if we keep our households in order and are kind to the stranger, fatherless and widow, xiv. 29. Thus we see that the five Books of Moses are all intended to regulate and make home happy. St. Paul says, "if any man hunger let him eat at home."—xi. of 1st Corin., 34 verse. In his Epistle to Titus women are desired "to be discreet chaste, keepers at home," ii. 5. St. Luke tells us there was a righteous priest and his wife, of the name of Zacharias and Elizabeth, who was one of the daughters of Aaron, walking in all the commandments of the Lord blameless. These pious people were chosen to have a son, who prepared the way for the coming of the Messiah, but see, although they led so pure a life they needed a miracle to open their eye of Faith, and the world seems now to require some miracle or sign to make them believe that goodness must prevail, which reminds me that Christ has said "When the Son of Man cometh shall he find faith on the earth."—Luke 18. 8. Moses says: "know therefore that the Lord thy God, he is God, the faithful God, which keepeth covenant and mercy with them that love him and keep his commandments to a thousand generations," Deuteronomy vii. 9, and he requires us to have a perfect faith in him, Deut. xxxii. 20. "God will hide his face" from "children in whom is no faith." All the men who were chosen of God to do his work were men of faith. After the Patriarchs look at Moses who God said himself "My servant Moses" who is faithful in all mine house."—Numbers xii. 7. God warned Eli, when his sons failed to do his work well, that he would raise up a faithful priest, which was fulfilled in Samuel, he acknowledged God in all his ways, and set up a stone saying, "Hitherto hath the

Lord helped us," 1st Sam. vii. 12, and St. Paul says in Hebrews xi. that time would fail to tell of the mighty works that have been wrought through the great Faith of the Patriarchs, Priests and Prophets, who have lived on the earth." All the people that the Saviour restored to health were possessed of great Faith, the three he raised to life were monuments of Faith. See how Jesus loved the little family of Bethany, and why Mary's words "Lord if thou hadst been here my brother had not died" shew that she believed that Jesus could have saved her brother's life if he had been there; but she had yet to learn that he could raise to life, and that as God he is every where present, so that he could have caused "that even this man should not have died" but he wished to open their eyes and ours, and to show that in his own good time he will stay the hand of death, and also raise to life with a glorified body those that have left the earth in Faith in him, but to hasten this time we must subdue ourselves and not be conformed to this world.—12 Romans 2. We must, like our Saviour, be kind and thoughtful for the feelings of others, ever striving to make those around us happy. Every hour of his life was spent in acts of kindness, not to one particular object or pet subject, but to all and every person that sought his assistance, and just as he raised the widow's son, Lazarus, and Jairus' daughter so will he raise every believer, convert every Jew and unite every christian church, and bring all to a state of perfect holiness here on earth. When the power of evil, which for six thousand years has bound the world in sin and selfishness, is chained, then what a paradise this earth will be! What a glorious time when we will have the privilege of walking in the garden like Adam with our Maker and talking to Jesus, hearing from his own lips the words "Go thou and preach the kingdom of God."—Luke ix. 60. The

Bible says plainly that we are to expect the Lord, for we are told to be always ready, none can tell when he will come. "Let your loins be girded about, and your lights burning, and ye yourselves like unto men that wait for their Lord."—Luke xii. 35. Nearly 1900 years ago the disciples were thus exhorted to wait; there were then but a few, very few christians, now about one third of the world are nominally christians. When the disciples asked Jesus, "Lord, wilt thou at this time restore again the kingdom to Israel," 1 Acts 6, he refused to satisfy their idle curiosity, but told them that they should bear witness to his work to all parts of the earth, and, though we are not allowed to know the times or seasons of his coming, still it is right to be always expecting. "Watch ye, therefore, for ye know not when the master of the house cometh."—Mark xiii. 35. Until the harvest we are told the good and bad are to grow together. David says: All the kindreds of the nations shall worship before thee.—Psalm xxii. 27. His rest shall be glorious.—Isaiah xi. 10; Micah iv. 4. But they shall sit every man under his vine and under his fig tree, and, 8th verse, and thou, O tower of the flock, the stronghold of the daughter of Zion, unto thee shall it come, even the first dominion. The kingdom shall come to the daughter of Jerusalem." ii. 12 says, surely I will gather the remnant of Israel with numberless others. One miracle we are distinctly told to look for at that time, in Isaiah xi. 15. The Lord shall utterly destroy the tongue of the Egyptian sea, and with his mighty wind, shall he shake his hand over the river, and shall smile in the seven streams and make men go over dry shod.

This prophecy may mean (remark the writer does not say that it does) but it may mean that the Lord will utterly destroy the sea of wickedness which has spread itself through the earth; that he will penetrate with his Spirit the most intricate windings of the secret paths of sin, and then smite those streams of selfishness which are drowning the souls of men, and lead us in the paths of holiness and peace, for Christ came that we might have life, yes that we might have it more abundantly. The devil's pride is so great that he has even said, I will ascend above the heights of the clouds, I will be like the Most High.—Isaiah xiv. 14. For this purpose he persuaded men to build the tower of Babel, whose top was to reach to Heaven. This tower, was no doubt a sort of round church, through which the devil persuaded men that they should gain the mansions of the blessed. But the great Spirit soon dispersed these vain ideas, and has been trying to teach men ever since that by no human stairs but only through faith in Jesus and obedience to his commands will that end be obtained. The time is coming when Satan and his works will be unveiled, then will be asked the question: "Is this the man that made the earth to tremble, that did shake kingdoms," xiv. 16. For some wise purpose he is allowed to indulge in his mad thoughts for a time, and to fill men's minds with the same. See, for example, how he has persuaded Professor Darwin to assert that man was originally a monkey, man, whose soul is offered the benefits of the sacrifice of a perfect human body with the Divine nature wherein to wash and be clean. An antidote for the poison which the evil Spirit has inserted in our veins, and yet clever men allow intellectual pride to be the ruin of their souls. Surely any trial, no matter how severe, that will teach us to know and feel the power of God and will subdue the pride of body or mind to the saving of the immortal part of our being, should be received thankfully and borne patiently, for the greatest improvements in science that can be made can only add a little more knowledge and comfort for a few fleeting years, but the victory of good over evil will cause to hear the "Great Voice saying, Behold the Tabernacle of God is with men, and he will dwell with them, and they shall be his people, and God himself shall be with them and be their God."—Rev. xxi. 3.

The many new devices that the evil Spirit is now using to keep mankind from loving the Great Creator draws our thoughts to the words of St. Paul to Timothy, now the Spirit speaketh expressly, that in the latter times some shall depart from the faith, giving heed to seducing spirits and doctrines of devils," 1 Tim. iv. 1, and Professor Darwin's theory, that man was originally a monkey, is without doubt, a doctrine of the evil Spirit. It is his object to conceal from us the fact that our souls can never die, and that two places are prepared to receive them. God has warned us that a fire "shall burn into the lowest Hell."—Deut. xxxii. 22. "Hell and destruction are never full."—Prov. xxvii. 20. "Hell hath enlarged herself and opened her mouth without measure."—Isaiah v. 14. And he has told us that "The fining pot is for silver and the furnace for gold, but the Lord trieth the hearts."—Prov. xvii. 3. Thus it is plain our own actions must determine the future state of the soul. We are free to choose this day whom we will serve.—Joshua xxiv. 15. In all great battles the soldiers fight for the cause they have espoused, so in this great war we fight either against the temptation of the evil Spirit and overcome by the help of the sword of the Spirit, and the armour of Faith, or we yield to the arts of the tempter and sink gradually and imperceptibly into his power when we find the oil of God's lamp gone out and our souls like a benighted traveller on a dark night who has lost his way seeking for the road from which we should never have strayed, for "the path of the just is as the shining light that shineth more and more unto the perfect day."—Prov. iv. 18, and it is only by walking in this path that we can become like the being Adam was before he sinned. "At that day shall a man look to his Maker, and his eyes shall have respect to the Holy One of Israel. And he shall not look to the altars the work of his hands, neither shall respect that which his fingers have made, either the groves or the images."—Isaiah xvii. 7, 8. And Ezekiel, in his 36th chap., sees this desolate earth once more looking "like the garden of Eden." In those days men will realize that there are four temples, not four religions, for the latter four will entwine themselves around the parent vine, and the birds of the air will lodge in the branches. 1st. All will then know Christ as the true temple. 2nd. Every believer as a living temple. 3rd. The gospel church as the mystical temple.—Eph .ii. 21. 4th. Heaven the everlasting temple. All will see the necessity for public and private prayer, both of which our Lord taught by example and precept. To public prayer he alluded when he said, " If two of you shall agree on earth as touching any thing that they shall ask, it shall be done for them of my Father which is in heaven, for where two or three are gathered together in my name, there am I in the midst of them."—Matt. xviii. 19. These words, an eminent Divine calls the "charters of public worship. In these we seem to approach God as a society incorporated by the royal charter of his Son, uniting in prayer for the same wants and petitions."

The beautiful liturgy of the Episcopal Church is suitable to the wants of all mankind, and it has the advantage of a perfect agreement between minister and people. There are times, no doubt, when extempore prayer is a benefit, but in the House of God minister and people are not agreed, unless both are uttering the same words at the same time. No one can know what the minister is going to say before he utters it. In the Romish mass the priest offers the mass for the people and prays for them in an unknown tongue, so they are not agreed. It thus follows that, if we fall short in practise, we have the greater cause for humiliation because the privilege both of the doctrine and discipline of prayer in which priest and people are both agreed is what Christ commands. But it is not sufficient that priest and people utter the same words at the same time; the hearts of both must be lifted with the words, to the throne of God; we must try to feel a holy reverence in His temple for the great God who condescends to allow us to worship in a house made with hands his great and glorious majesty. Our first aim should be to realize that God is everywhere, in earth, and sky, and sea, and though not now visibly present in the temple, as he appeared in the Shekinah to the Jews, still he clothed himself with a perfect human body and dwelt among men, to show us that from childhood to manhood we may overcome evil with good, and, though he has withdrawn his human body from the earth, His Holy Spirit communes with our spirit in the bread and wine at his own table, exactly in the same way as it did in that glorious Sight in which he spoke to man from off the mercy seat, "Take eat this is my Body" "This is my blood of the New Testament.—" Mark xiv. 22, 24. Remark that Christ does not say that he changes the bread and wine into his body and blood, but that he inhabits it. His Spirit is to be found in it by the use of a perfect faith, and the soul that has had the spirit of goodness planted in it through the waters of baptism, has renewed and strenghtened these vows at the hands of a bishop in confirmation, and is constantly fed, at regular and stated periods, with the Holy Fire in the bread and wine, will, through this perfect faith, daily increase in holiness and in the knowledge of the Lord.

Ezra says, that the Tirshatha "said unto them that they should not eat of the most holy things till there stood up a priest with Urim and with Thummim.— Ezra, ii. 63. This was something attached to the breast plate by which the mind of God was made known to the high priest when enquired of them in cases of difficulty. Now Christ was that priest, he both knew and did the will of God; therefore the time has come for us to eat of holy things as allowed by the Tirshatha. Spiritual life requires spiritual food to sustain it. All creeds and all nations can agree to supply their bodily wants; at the same market all feed and dress their bodies with the richest and best, at regular and stated intervals; but alas! how divided how careless, how unsettled, are the arrangements for the nourishment of the soul—that soul which is always progressing either in good or evil! It may be that it has three progressive states, finding perfection only when found worthy to become an angel in the third heaven. The first state of trial, the present, which is passing rapidly away. The second the place to which our Lord descended when his Holy Spirit left his perfect body, which groaned under the separation, for it exclaimed, "My God my God why hast thou forsaken me.—Mat. xxvii. 46. It is the body that speaks, the soul and spirit travel to that unknown land but are speechless, Christ went then to the place where our spirits go when they leave the body. It cannot be that they there enjoy the presence of God; for after Christ rose from the grave he told Mary not to touch him for he had not yet ascended to his Father, then he shewed himself " alive after his passion by many infallible proofs being seen of them forty days and speaking of the things pertaining to the kingdom of God."—Acts, i. 3; and this kingdom will be the third and last place of trial, or perhaps preparation would be a better word, for the glory which awaits us. Isaiah says, men have not heard nor perceived by the ear, neither hath the eye seen, O God, besides thee, what he hath prepared for him that waiteth for Him.—" Isaiah lxiv. 4. The three first chapters in the Bible shew what misery Adam brought on the human race by listening to the suggestions of the Evil Spirit. The three last chapters in the Bible show what happiness he will regain when he follows the guidance of the Good Spirit. The Evil Spirit does not give us even a few years of perfect happiness in return for all our service. The influence of the Good Spirit causes the Soul to do good and great works which are always like the even and regular ebbings of the tide returning to the mind with pleasing and happy thoughts, bringing to it peace and contentment, which speaks of something lasting, something great to be obtained from a loving and heavenly Father. Earthly parents spoil their children by over-indulgence, they fail in not teaching them that this earth is yet a divided kingdom, and that earthly desires are not always to be granted, the consequences are that the pleasing of the body is the ruling passion. Thus the body becomes unaccustomed to any act of self denial and unprepared to deny itself any fancied pleasure. Those who do sell their souls for the gratification of any evil passion have but little enjoyment. Thus the drunkard finds pleasure in drinking, but how does he feel when he is sober. The miser finds pleasure in his gold, how does he feel when he loses it or leaves it. The sharper finds pleasure in cheating you, if he gains but a few dollars by the act, how does he feel when he thinks of the account of his stewardship which he must one day give. The smuggler is delighted if by concealing some lace and gloves on his person he can deceive the officer, by so doing he may deceive them, but does he thus think to deceive his God, alas, no!—

"All things are naked and opened unto the eyes of him with whom we have to do."- Heb. iv. 13. But goodness though slandered, abused, and despised sees in the distance the city that "had no need of the sun, neither of the moon, to shine in it; for the glory of God did lighten it and the Lamb is the light thereof."—Rev. xxi. 23, and feels the cross light that leads him to the gates, those gates which Christ will open to those that approach the Father through him, for he has said "I am the way, the truth and the life. The wicked do not enjoy the company of the good, even in the present state of the world, how can they hope to enjoy a city "that there shall in no wise enter into it any thing that defileth, neither whatsoever worketh abomination or maketh a lie."—Rev. xxi. 27. Christians are now like a house divided against itself, our Lord warned us that such a house cannot stand. If the great struggle of good and evil is at hand, the Devil is preparing his spirits to "go forth unto the kings of the earth and of the whole world, to gather them to the battle of that great day of God Almighty."—Rev. xvi. 14. And he gathered them to that place called in the Hebrew tongue Armageddon. None can tell where this place is or when this battle will be fought, but we are told in the Bible that the result of it is to be the complete overthrow of the power of the evil Spirit; he and all his works are to be destroyed and withdrawn from this beautiful earth. With this end so clearly before us it especially behoves us to try and come to some united belief on the subject of sacramental rites and ordinances. Some very pious and clever persons believe that there are seven sacraments, some say there are five, some allow there may be three, our church teaches two only as generally necessary to salvation. The word sacrament is not to be found in the Bible, but our souls must require food as well as our bodies to sustain them, and Christ, both by precept and example, enforced the need of certain means which we must use if we wish to be washed in his blood. Baptism and Christ's own supper are as it were the principal of these, but God himself instituted Matrimony, it must, therefore be a sacrament. Confimation, it is true, was not actually commanded by Christ, but then it was the custom in the early church, and is as it were a part of Baptism and so must partake of its nature. It says in Acts viii. 16, 17, "Only they were baptized in the name of the Lord Jesus, then laid they their hands on them and they received the Holy Ghost." Every ordinance by which the soul receives spiritual food or life from the Holy Spirit of God must be sacramental, for a sacrament is really spiritual food, for they are the channels through which our spiritual life must flow, and when we partake of them in God's own way Christ will give us of the living water which the poor woman of Samaria had within her reach but failed to acquire. At present we are fulfilling faithfully the picture Christ described "five in one house divided, three against two, and two against three."— Luke xii. 52. All, whether Indians, Turks or Hottentots, have immortal souls, but observe the effect of Baptism on the soul. Even those who have planted but not watered that seed with the other sacraments are more civilized, they have at least made one step in the right road. The sun, moon and stars all give us light, none can tell exactly which of these produces it because it is a thing that comes from God himself. We see plainly that as the body is constituted it needs the light of all these as also the sky to contain them, and the air to convey the light to us; the loss of any one of them would seriously affect us. Thus also is the light of the soul transmitted to us. The sun and moon, like Baptism and the Lord's supper, are absolutely necessary. The stars attending on the moon, like Confirmation following Baptism. The sky represents Matrimony, the air ordination, for it is through the priesthood that the sacraments are administered to us. This seems to prove plainly what I stated at the beginning, that light and goodness come from the good Spirit, darkness and wickedness from the evil Spirit, and as all God's works are regular and united in their movements, so if we wish to please him and to have him to reign over us we must become one on these doctrinal points and "worship the father in spirit and in truth."—John iv. 23. One can hardly realize any one accepting the office of a priest without feeling that the ordinance which fits him for that office is a sacrament requiring both study and close communion with God such as Moses and Aaron enjoyed. It was Christ himself who first appeared as a priest under the name of Melchizadec, then God called Aaron to be a prophet, Ex. vii. 1, or as he is afterwards called a priest; his successors continued in office till our Saviour came, they perhaps do still in the Jewish church. Then came our Saviour in human form, and though not visible he is still our great High Priest; but his chosen twelve apostles and seventy disciples left their successors who from generation to generation have filled, and do still fill the priestly office in the christian church. "The gates of hell have not prevailed against" the three churches which St. Peter planted and the branches which have sprung from them. The commission that Christ gave them was, "Go ye unto all the world and preach the Gospel to every creature," Mark xvi. 15, and St. Matthew gives it, "Go ye therefore and teach all nations, baptising them in the name of the Father and of the Son and of the Holy Ghost." Here their work is clearly set down to teach and pre ch and baptize, had Christ given them power to forgive sins it would have been mentioned here. It is true that St. John in his 20th chapter says that Christ, after bestowing on the apostles the Holy Ghost, said, "Whosoever sins ye remit they are remitted unto them and whosoever sins ye retain they are retained." But had this been intended to give them some extraordinary power of forgiving sins he would surely have explained it also to Thomas, for he was not with them, and did not believe that Christ had risen; but Jesus convinced him of his want of faith by shewing him the print of the nails and the hole in his side, and Thomas exclaimed at once "my Lord and my God," making Thomas, by his public confession, an example of what Christ required, viz., that we should, in the words of a public confession such as is found in our prayer book, confess our sins before God, and then the priest has the power to give a general absolution such as the one that follows it. But the consequence of sin is death. That, no priest has the power to destroy. The Jews believed that none could forgive sins but God alone.—Mark ii. 7. Christ tried to teach them that he was divine and had the power to drive away sin from the earth. As soon as he desired the man sick of the palsy to rise, "He arose, took the bed and went forth before them all."—Mark ii. 12. And as soon as he speaks the word the christian church which is now shaking with the palsy will unite and encircle the whole earth.

The body of Christ was made "perfect through suffering."—Heb. ii. 10. Christians and Christianity are undergoing a trial of affliction to fit them for greater happiness than man has ever known. Every thing worldly ends in death but the hope of the christian is life, and the triumph of christianity will be the destruction of Death. The saints in heaven are said to have come through much tribulation.—Rev. vii. 14. They have encountered the evil Spirit and conquered him. What they have done with the help of God's Holy Spirit we can do. But we never will conquer death till we destroy our idol and its worship. Idolatry never flourished more among the Jews than it does now among christians. Go to our christian meetings, what is the chief topic of conversation? It is money. A savage suddenly transported from his wilds to one of our assemblies with the power of understanding our language, would suppose that money, not God's glory, was the chief end of man. The evil Spirit now holds such sway over the hearts of men that he makes both ministers and people believe that with money they can buy their soul's salvation. Congregations say, we pay the money, we shall have for our minister the one we choose. These monied men that do him worship say this minister must honor us, and in general they do. In their eagerness to obtain the cursed thing, all seem to forget that God has promised to give what is needful to those that trust in him, and he will both provide the individual and the church that labors and trusts all its wants to him. They need have no fears while they do their duty and what their conscience tells them is right. God sometimes tries christians sorely, demands all and every thing that we value to see of what our faith is made, whether we really believe that he has the power which can make all things work together for our good or whether our faith is a dead faith, trusting only in human aids and human gifts. We are free agents in the choice of good or evil, and though the banner that waves around us sometimes conceals even from ourselves the side on which we are fighting, yet the smallest action of our lives serves some great and allwise purpose, and is gradually preparing us either for an angel of light or of darkness. Christ has taught us the necessity of love and charity between all christians, "By this shall all men know that ye are my disciples. If ye have love one to another."—John xiii. 35. "One is your master, even Christ, and all ye are brethren," Matthew xxiii. 8, and his prayer that they all may be one, John xvii. 21, will yet, I believe, restore sweet and holy communion between all the christian churches. It is certain that such love did exist in the early ages of the Church before earthly ambition and unchristian feelings were planted by the evil Spirit. We read that Peter was accompanied by six brethren when he went to Cornelius, Acts xi. 12, and when Paul departed from Ephesus to go to Macedonia we are told that he had with him, "Sopater of Berea, and of the Thessalonians Aristarchus and Secundus; and Gaius of Derbe, and Timotheus; and of Asia, Tychicus and Trophimus.—Acts xx. 4. In the three last verses of this chapter we read that they prayed together and wept very sore at parting from Paul, for they felt that they should see his face no more. Then in the apostles' time christians admitted to their communion those who came from other countries, they contributed to the relief of distressed believers in all parts, and they exchanged letters and advice. "A bishop in those days, quoted from early history, could give any member of his church a letter which when presented would admit him into all the privileges of christian fellowship. We have in the epistle of St. Clement, Bishop of Rome and the Roman church, addressed to the Church of Corinth before the end of the first century on occasion of a schism in the latter church, an instance of fraternal intercourse and solicitude. And in the following centuries, the epistle of Dyonisius, Bishop of Corinth, to many churches in Pontus, Crete, and that of the Council of Antioch to all the churches are further examples of the same practice. We learn that even in the second century, the Church of Rome was remarkable for the extent of its charities to the distressed and persecuted christians in the East, and Dyonisius of Alexandria, in the following century, attests that the same truly christian conduct was still in full exercise, and its benefits were felt even in the remote regions of Arabia." 'Tis true that even in St. Paul's time the Church of Corinth was full of parties and divisions, for even Paul and Barnabas had a sharp contention and separated.—Acts xv. 39. Though they may have had different opinions on some subjects they felt one common bond of interest in their christian work. St. Paul exhorted them to remember that Christ was not divided, and St. Jude says, those "who separate themselves are sensual, having not the Spirit." — If we divide man's sojourn on earth into periods, the first including the time which elapsed from the creation to the deluge, we find that men grew gradually worse and worse till God swept him off the earth by a flood and then repeopled the earth again through Noah and his three sons, four men whose descendants soon forgot the great display of power which the Almighty had shown by covering the earth with water, and filled with pride conceived the idea of building the church or tower of Babel. Then God, we are told, came down, and, by confounding their language, scattered them over the whole earth. Then follows the call of Abraham whose descendants God made his peculiar care. God watched over them, guarded them, guided them, and fed them directly from heaven, and yet they failed to worship him as he wished to be worshipped. Then Christ came on earth as a Saviour, which is the fourth period. "He came unto his own and his own received him not."—John i. 11. The Jews were his own chosen ones, but they were too proud to believe that God could condescend to come on earth in the humble manner in which Christ came; and now if we are on the eve of a fifth period let us not, like our forefathers, sink our ship on the rock of pride, but, uniting in christian love and charity, may we sail out into the beautiful clear blue waters, and with strong faith at the helm we will yet lay hold on the Tree of Life. But at present we are all suffering from this disease. The Jew cannot yet see that the world has been redeemed. Christians do not believe that God will soon glorify it. When the Holy Ghost descended upon the apostles " they were all with one accord in one place."—Acts ii. 1. So that they, at least, then must have been united. Has not the Almighty yet shown us enough of his power? Why is it we cannot see that he is determined that we shall learn to know him through the eye of faith, such faith as will teach us to feel that he can make man a perfect being, that he can eject the poison of evil from his veins, and drive sin from this beautiful earth. In 1851, when Prince Albert, your beloved earthly parent, drew together all the nations of the earth for a display of industry, did not man show the greatness of his intellect and the wonderful power of the mind that God has given him; what would not that mind produce when united in the great Christian cause? Those whose privilege it was to feast their senses on the beautiful structure, designated the Crystal Palace of Concord, in which the brotherhood of nations was celebrated—who gazed on the various works of art which filled up and decorated that earthly temple and greeted with acclamations of joy our beloved Queen and her illustrious consort, for planning and labouring to engage the intelligence and mechanical genius of all nations—should consider what a far greater work is waiting one great master-mind, the united efforts of body and soul, to prepare the world for the reign of Christ upon earth. The skilful manner in which the Germans conducted their war with France prove plainly that, if such a nation could be induced to unite in promoting our great eternal interests, and make a great effort for the union of the Christian churches, the millennium would begin to dawn on the earth,—that time when Christ "shall come to be glorified in his saints, and admired in all them that believe.—" 2nd Thes. i. 10. Christians are now indeed a stumbling block through their divisions. St. Paul's warning has been unheeded "Take heed lest by any means this liberty of yours become a stumbling block to them that are weak."— 1st Cor. viii. 9. Christ, as prophesied by Isaiah, is the stumbling stone, that they, the Jews, the builders, have rejected,—"And he shall be for a sanctuary; but for a stone of stumbling and for a rock of offence to both the houses of Israel."—Isa. viii. 14; and pause and consider if our divisions are a stumbling block to the Jews. God has threatened to consume the stumbling blocks with the wicked.—Zeph. i. 3, and in in the 14th verse it says: "The great day of the Lord is near and hasteth greatly." They are, therefore, to be destroyed before the reign of Christ; and the 18th verse says, "neither their silver nor their gold shall be able to deliver them in the day of the Lord's wrath! St. John was permitted to see in a vision the marriage of the Lamb, the encircling of the Christian Church with a marriage ring.—Rev. xix. 7. We are told that Christ will then find five wise virgins, and five foolish ones without oil in their lamps. May the Christian Church soon begin to trim her lamps for he comes and is near. "Blessed and holy is he that hath part in the first resurrection; on such the second death hath no power, but they shall be priests of God and of Christ, and shall reign with him a thousand years." It thus seems quite plain that we are to look forward to two resurrections, one before the thousand years and one after; those who have the privilege of coming back to this earth with a glorified body will meet the Lord in the air at the judgment day, for St. Paul says that " the Lord himself shall descend from Heaven with a shout, with the voice of the archangel, and with the trump of God and the dead in Christ shall rise first.— 1st Thes. iv. 16. Then the kingdoms of this world are become the kingdoms of our Lord, and of his Christ, and he shall reign for ever and ever."—Rev. xi. 15.

Councils and Synods have been the means of doing much harm to the Christian Church. They have raised up among ministers feelings of pride and passion, making them wish for high-sounding names and high positions, which has taken from them much of that respect which the office requires, and given the laity a power which they never should have had in God's house.

ON SYNODS.

It gives me pain, indeed, to see
    Synods making useless laws;
They seem to meet to disagree,
    Quibbling about little flaws.

Are not the rules God Moses gave,
    And which Christ alone did teach,
Enough both priests and all to save ?
    Hear and heed them I beseech.

Christ told us other laws were vain,
    All traditions He forbid ;
But them he said we must maintain
    And then walk as Moses did.

Mankind lives but to break these laws
    Generations come and go,
Feeding Death's ever open jaws—
    Satan walking to and fro.

>These Canons that our Synods make
>Do not check him in the least;
>He smiles as each new law is cast;
>On men's doctrines he does feast.

God should be a Bishop's only adviser, and from him he will receive all that is necessary to advance him and his flock in the paths of holiness, for Christ has said "Lo, I am with you always." Let Bishops, Priests and Deacons meet together at times for the breaking of bread with prayer and praise, and their hearts will become more and more fitted for the reign of Christ. It is possible that the seventh thousand year of the world may be the Sabbath of the Lord, the rest for the righteous before they are caught up in the clouds to be ever with the Lord, for though God sees us and knows us, each and all, we will need some time to prepare us to worship God in his heavenly temple. The Lord informed Moses, Ex. xix. 6, that this people should "Be unto him a kingdom of priests and an holy nation." Daniel says, "that the saints of the Most High shall possess the kingdom prepared for you from the foundation of the world." This seems to infer that this world was intended to be the kingdom of the righteous, yes, and they will yet obtain possession of it.

Dear Christian Princess, I have addressed you in this letter without the etiquette which is your due, because I feel that in such a spiritual work there is no need of ceremony. I have drawn your attention in this letter to the great points of contention among Christians; but the key note on which all the harmony depends is the three-fold essence of our great Creator, which is truly a mystery, but still a right knowledge of it is necessary to our salvation. Plato, who lived 360 years before the Christian era, taught his disciples that there were three persons in the Godhead, the Supreme Good, the mind and the soul.

I have no doubt that the early Christians, who saw Christ's divinity in his actions, had no contentions on this subject, but were all united in its views, for this was the principal feature that distinguished them from the Jews of that time. The Greek Church, whose link is not yet broken, appears to have preserved this doctrine in its purest state, the Three all equal and co-eternal. Moses tells us we are made after God's own image, and we are quite conscious of having a body, mind, and soul, or spirit, for we feel within us the power of thought, and also a sort of electric communion with the Great Being who directs all our ways. You will see that I have, in the other parts of the book, tried to make this, and all the other points on which Christians contend, as plain as verse can make them, and if through God's blessing you, and the German people, can be induced to take an interest in the work, I may hope that it will sow the seed of Christian unity whose first blossom will be the conversion of the Jewish people to the acknowledgment of Christ as the Messiah, who then will return as King of kings and Lord of lords; when they will once more enjoy that sweet intercourse with Jehovah which it was the privilege of the Fathers to entertain. "And the Lord will create upon every dwelling place of Mount Zion and upon her assemblies a cloud of smoke by day, and the shining of a flaming fire by night, for upon all the glory shall be a defence, and there shall be a Tabernacle for a shadow in the day time from the heat and for a place of refuge." That you may be one of those of whom St. John writes as follows is the sincere wish of the writer of this letter.

Seven promises our Lord has made
    To those who overcome,
And ev'ry word that He has said
    Most surely will be done.

The tree that from man's sight was hid,
    When he first disobey'd,
Will in our gardens grow amid
    The fruit that man betray'd.

The second death no pow'r shall have
    On these His favor'd ones,
Their bodies glorified shall live,
    And wear the crown they've won.

With hidden manna God will feed,
    A white stone will obtain,
This stone, his passport, none shall read,
    But him who it does name.

Nations shall be ruled by him,
    Who, faithful to the end,
Controls and keeps himself from sin,
    When Satan does contend.

He shall be cloth'd in raiment white,
    His sins all wash'd away,
His new name Christ will bring to light
    And glorify his clay.

A pillar in God's temple seen,
    No more to be displac'd,
Three glorious names will on Him gleam,
    When sin is all effac'd.

A throne is for such saints prepar'd
    With Christ on earth to reign,
A palace free from pain or care,
    Then love all hearts will chain.

OUR FIRST PARENTS.

Adam and Eve a lesson teach,
To which attention I beseech;
Reflect mankind, this happy pair
Were placed in Eden free of care.

The earth all drest in beauteous green
Blooming fruits around are seen;
To work and keep, to taste and eat,
To be of living things the chief.

One little thing his God forbid—
The reason was from Adam hid—
God gave him all that he did need,
And yet he stole the little seed.

Week after week man steals the rest
God has chosen man's faith to test;
Sun, moon and stars their God obey
Move on and on from day to day.

But man spurns all his Maker's love,
And welcomes not the Heavenly Dove.
What more could man or woman want
Than God to tie the marriage knot?

Adam and Eve did not this prize,
But thought to be like God's more wise;
They tasted of the hidden fruit,
Which made them blind and deaf and mute.

If Eve had trusted in her God,
And bid the serpent fear his rod,
Made Adam noble, wise and great,
How happy then the marriage state.

God's glory all around to cheer,
What need would they have had to fear,
Their bodies ne'er have turned to dust
Nor out of Paradise been thrust.

Thunder and lightning never heard,
But angels singing like the birds,
Clouds ne'er have floated o'er the sky
Nor tears bedew'd man's lovely eye.

The earth would never then have quak'd,
Nor fire beneath have made her shake,
Man's body never known a pain,
Nor ever hid from God with shame.

Our infant days without a tear,
Nor ever cradled in a bier,
Childhood's gay hopes, and happy song
Have cheer'd us all our lives along.

Our weekly rest and daily toil
Have girded man with virtue's coil,
He selfish then would not have been
Every Eve have been a queen.

Each to the other would have brought
Holy love and heavenly thought,
God's glory been their chief delight
And with him walked by day and night.

Our spirits, daily fed with grace,
Would ne'er have sought another place,
No souls to Satan have been bound
To follow him for ever round.

But all our bodies, spirits, souls
Must pray the angel with live coals
Our lips to touch, our mouths to cleanse,
Ere Jesus to this earth descends.

Now women, maidens see how Eve
Herself and Adam did deceive!
'Tis time her children should awake
Some new and great endeavors make.

To banish death from this our land
For we are now but bags of sand;
Time wearing all and each away,
Our life is but a little day.

United all in one strong band,
Evil to crush on every hand;
Never to flirt, deceive nor lie,
Then Death will take his wings and fly.

A little band I'll surely find
Who to God's rules themselves will bind,
Without regard to church and state,
Or thinking what's to be their fate;

Will trust to God in each event,
And do each duty as its sent,
Each in the home where God has placed,
No matter how those duties taste;

The Sabbath in his temple spend
To pray him every blessing send.
The Tree of Life God then will give
And we eternally will live.

Two Spirits now our bodies hold,
For to evil we have been sold;
But Christ has bought us for his own,
Wash'd in his blood we shall be known.

When this kingdom Christ comes to claim
Satan himself to bind and chain,
Man will not then good people shun,—
They will his kings and priests become.

Hasten Oh Lord! this blessed time,
Send down some great some wondrous sign,
To cause thy people to unite
And worship thee with all their might!

THE SECOND EVE.

The Blessed Virgin now behold,
Her pictures always hung in gold,
Some do adore, some worship, them,
And artists make her their great gem.

But Oh! how was it when on earth
Ere she to Jesus did give birth?
What shame and sorrow, sadness, woe,
Was her portion here below.

An angel had from heaven to come
To tell her husband fear to shun;
The power of the Holy One
A perfect human body won.

No palace then was open'd wide
Where she her lovely babe could hide,
But in a manger he was laid—
A stable was her only shade.

'Tis plain she but a woman was,
Endow'd with wisdom for the cause;
Eve's purest daughter good and chaste
Of all earth's trials here did taste.

She knew her Son was all divine,
She saw in him two natures shine;
All round her she bid him obey—
Be sure you do what he does say.

She learnt to love him and to fear
May we like her his words revere
She never gave us any sign,
To make us think *She* was divine.

Eve as a Spirit God did see
And then in fire appeared he
Surely God could as Jesus come
His work on earth himself have done.

THE SABBATH EVE.

How sweet and peaceful is the rest
   Of the Christian's Sabbath eve,
Sweet foretaste of the holiness
   Which will us soon from sin relieve.

Our pleasures then not mixed with pain,
   All our sorrows turn'd to joy;
Christians, then, in more than name,
   Our souls in virtue will employ.

No thistles then will grow apace,
   No thorns to pierce one's very heart;
The earth will then begin to taste
   The sweetness plann'd in God's great chart.

Truth then will shine in every place,
   Faith will be our guiding star;
God's glory glowing in each face,
   And nothing to annoy or jar.

Beauty, then, the eye will behold,
   And in virtue all will be drest,
Bright gems and pearls and wealth untold,
   Will be shining on each breast.

Our eyes will never lose their sight,
   No deafness will our ears offend,
Our hair be glossy, teeth be white
   Our youthful days will never end.

Then all will learn that "God is love,"
   His wisdom all will then perceive,
The patience of the Holy Dove,
   And mercy that could Christ receive.

As an atonement for man's sin,
   The fallen angels to replace,
That when man heav'n enters in,
   He may not like them lose his place.

How great the God that shows such love
   To wilful, wicked, sinful men,
Who always watches from above,
   And bids the angel take a pen.

And each and ev'ry holy act,
   Down in the Book of Life he writes,
And promises to read these facts,
   As soon as Satan takes his flight,

With all those who have worship'd him,
   To the region now call'd hell,
There they will live with him in sin,
   In torment there for ever dwell.

No Sabbath rest for such as these,
   They will in that time be withdrawn,
But to return when Christ shall please,
   To call them on the judgment morn.

Come then, beware, at once prepare
   A rest is waiting for the blest,
A Sabbath eve of virtues rare,
   With peace and love will all be drest.

JEWISH ALTAR.

On the sanctuary where Jehovah dwelt
    The guardian cherubims spread their wings,
'Mid golden flowers, trees and fruit man felt,
    He might have heard the very angels sing.

When first with God's glory the altar shone,
    How wonderful man did not then obey,
And seek at once for his sins to atone,
    Through the great High Priest in God's chosen way.

But nothing so strong as man's stubborn will,
    With evil he delights to be guided,
It pleases him best to do what is ill,
    And never yet in God has confided.

Aaron, the priest, made an idol of gold,
    This image made Moses' anger wax hot,
The tables of stone he dropt from his hold,
    Provok'd, his God's commands he forgot.

To man at first God spake them from above,
    Then wrote them with his finger on the stone,
But, ever good, call'd Moses, and in love
    He bid him write those words with him alone.

To keep these rules quite pure God gave some laws,
    A schoolmaster, to draw us near to Christ
When man these rules does practise, then the jaws
    Of death will close in this our paradise.

Christ kept these laws from childhood to the grave;
    He led a life obedient and kind;
No longer let the devil make us slaves,
    And with his sins our souls and bodies bind.

To make us his in misery and woe,
   To cheat us of our heritage and right,
To make us serve him here, and then below,
   He hides from us God's glories pure and bright.

O! let us then at once destroy his chains,
   With patience wear the cross our father sends;
With wisdom and with love it was ordained,
   To fit us all for joys that have no end.

For ear hath never heard nor eye hath seen,
   The joy for those that taste the Tree of Life,
That city which St. John just had a gleam,
   This kingdom where God's glory is the light.

A POEM

ON THE THREE-FOLD ESSENCE OF GOD

A The Ark.   C The Candlestick.   G The Shekinah.
N The Altar of Incense.   T The Tabernacle.

THE CREATOR.

The Mighty One and Great I AM,
The whole universe can span;
He moves upon the vasty deep—
All the orbs in order keep.

God did Himself to mankind give
This great world in which we live,
With all its creatures, fruits, and trees,
All on earth, in sky, and seas.

These, when God did for man provide,
With a woman by his side,
Were perfect, good, and blooming bright,
A grand and glorious sight.

With this Great Being they did walk,
And God then to them did talk,
They knew not what it was to fear,
When they His commands did hear.

His Providence still guards and guides,
Watches over man and child,
Though sin now hides Him from our sight,
All do feel His power and might.

Fresh air surrounds us night and day,
Sun and moon, with constant ray,
Causing the earth to reproduce
Food and fruits for mankind's use.

Trees with leaves of various hue,
Drops of rain and pearly dew,
The ebbing tide and gentle flow,
Hoary frost, and pure white snow.

The lightning which obeys His word,
Peals of thunder often heard,
The earth itself when it does quake,
Now with terror makes men shake.

The rapids with majestic roar,
Proud St. Lawrence, at our shore,
Whose waters join the river near,
Never mix, though through we steer.

Like good and evil in the world,
Both these banners are unfurl'd,
If men the former wish to be,
They must from the latter flee.

All that the universe contains
Proves that God Almighty reigns,
But above these, the link, the chain,
To make Holy once again.

Man, who in His own image made,
God, his Maker, disobey'd,
Is so merciful, just and wise,
That we His commands should prize.

Unseen His Spirit dwells within,
Those who struggle against sin,
The everlasting arm sustains,
When Christ's blood runs through the veins.

O ! What a great and wondrous plan,
To restore lost fallen man,
Love, mercy, justice, in it shine,
Flowing down through Christ the vine.

OUR REDEMPTION.

When Hagar fled from Abram's house,
    To the wilderness she stray'd,
Then, first, was heard the angel's voice,
    He pitied her and sav'd.

He gave her water from the well,
    And rais'd her thoughts on high,
The trials all which her befel
    Form'd a new and sacred tie.

When Abraham put forth his hand,
    With the knife his son to slay,
Then next appear'd in this fair land,
    The Angel Man, Christ our stay.

To him he spake the cheering words,
    "In thy seed shall all be bless'd,"
Behold the ram caught by his horns,
    This sacrifice was the test.

Of thy obedience, faith and love,
    Thou fearest God, that now I know,
His voice then told him from above,
    This faith will a good seed sow:

Giving the treasures of the heart,
    Yielding up the dearest thing,
Will give our enemy a start,
    And save us many a sting.

In crosslike form on Joseph's lads,
    See Jacob's hands are stretched out,
Imploring from the one who had
    Redeemed, blessings without count.

When Israel their feast did hold,
   In Gilgal, near Jericho,
Joshua did himself behold
   This Angel as he did go.

Then on his face he quickly fell
   And worshipp'd him as his Lord;
Holy the place he did him tell:
   Joshua obey'd His word.

To Manoah's wife this Angel came,
   Very terrible his mien,
Did wondrous things, and in the flame,
   He ascended from the scene.

When David fell in Satan's snare,
   And disobey'd his God,
His eyes beheld this Angel there,
   Staying the Avenging Rod.

He gently to Elijah spake,
   When he found him sad and lone;
The mountains rent, the earth did shake,
   But he heard that soft sweet tone.

Thus we see in the days of old,
   The Angel of His presence
Was the Guardian of His fold,
   And love His very essence.

Nebuchadnezzar, in his rage,
   Cast three Jews into the flames,
Good men, who were so very sage,
   Nothing could their honor stain.

This King a golden image made,
    To which all were bid to bow.
These worshipp'd God alone, they said;
    That they loudly would avow.

The King drew near this furnace hot,
    Unhurt these three men he sees;
But with them is the Son of God,
    Who from death and fire frees.

Not a hair of their head was sing'd,
    Their clothes did not smell of fire;
On them was not the slightest tinge
    Of harm from this King's ire.

Thus will it be on earth with man,
    When his ways are all upright;
The Angel who was Christ the Lamb,
    Will show his power and might.

Darius issued in his realm,
    What he thought a firm decree,
That none for thirty days should own
    Any God or King save he.

For if they did, they should be cast
    At once into a lion's den.
When this statute royal was pass'd,
    The King signed it with his pen.

Daniel, who feared God alone,
    Went into his house, and prayed
Three times a day, as he was prone,
    Before the decree was made.

In the morn, the King rose in haste,
    And went to the den to see
If this man, so wise and chaste,
    Could really living be.

The mouths of the lions were shut,
    The Angel of God was there;
So Daniel was taken up;
    His accusers in despair

Were cast with their children and wives
    To the lions, who devour'd.
No Angel came to save their lives,
    At once they felt their power.

Thus is it now, and so will be,
    With all those who Christ disown,
Evil from earth can never flee,
    Till this Angel Christ alone

Can make the Jewish people bend,
    And in Him Messiah see;
To Him the Branch they must attend,
    And fall low upon the knee.

Then shall all his neighbour call,
    Under the fig tree and vine;
Man and earth as before the Fall,
    Will labour and love entwine.

Redemption's work, so long begun,
    Christ finished on the Cross;
None but God's dear and only Son
    Could have paid the price it cost.

But it is paid ; the work is done,
    And Faith is the balance sheet ;
Christ's blood our Passover has won,
    For us grace and mercy meet.

A king and prophets all foretold
    The events which Christ fulfilled ;
Of David's line we him behold,
    And with lamb-like meekness filled.

His Mother was a Virgin fair,
    In Bethlehem He was born;
Of humble birth, with virtues rare,
    Then the star of Jacob shone.

From Herod He was forc'd to hide,
    For this star brought jealous fears ;
In Galilee he did reside,
    Till an angel voice he hears.

Sorrow, trial and temptation,
    Assail'd Him each day and hour ;
In every situation,
    He show'd almighty power.

When oppress'd and afflicted,
    His mouth he opened not ;
Of no sin was He convicted,
    For His vesture they cast lots.

With the wicked He met His death,
    In the rich man's tomb was laid ;
And is not this what Scripture saith?
    For a ransom should be paid.

But now behold the victory:
   Death has no power to keep,
We learn from Jesus' history,
   That He rose as from a sleep.

With body changed and glorified,
   His Disciples heard Him talk;
In Him, man's nature deified,
   Again on this earth did walk.

When Redemption's work was done,
   A cloud hid Him from our sight;
But when the time is fully come,
   Christ's glory will be light.

O, may a blessing now descend
   On this little work of love;
May each Christian to it lend
   The patience of the Dove.

Soon may Christians of all creeds
   Unite their Faith together,
Planting the Truth without the weeds,
   Living in Love for ever.

Then Death, the dreadful curse of sin,
   Will not wear our flesh away;
The power of the Serpent's sting,
   Christ, our antidote, will stay.

THE HOLY SPIRIT.

Behold! this earth all darkness reigns,
   God's spirit moves and all is light:
It open'd out earth's richest veins,
   And show'd our Maker's power and might.

His word, with an electric charm,
   Pierc'd through the gloom and brought forth light
Encircles earth and guards from harm,
   Gave birth to Adam and his wife.

All happy in a garden, they,
   With God's spirit, good and true,
Roam'd about from day to day,
   And nothing dark nor evil knew,

Till Eve the Serpent's voice beguil'd,
   To taste the tree that God forbid;
This sin brought death to man and child,
   And the Good Spirit from us hid.

Sin spread itself, till once again
   The earth was altogether dark;
For forty days a constant rain
   Drown'd all but those within the Ark.

For ten long months and forty days,
   Light never shed on earth a beam
Of its life-giving growth and rays,
   For water cover'd every seam.

Then once again, for mankind's sake,
   The Spirit caus'd the earth to yield;
To Noah in the Ark God spake,
   And fruitful soon was man and field.

God then a covenant made with man,
   The token of it is a bow,
Which always does the heavens span;
   Lights, varied colors in a row.

Thus when the earth baptised had been,
  A sacramental sign God gave,
That light from earth He would not screen,
  And man from evil He would save.

Then as a Priest the Spirit came;
  Bread and wine, our spiritual food,
With blessing He to Abram gave,
  And told him that he always should

Possessor be of Heaven and earth;
  Now beasts, and birds, and fishes all,
Assist Him in His joy and mirth,
  And are obedient to His call.

In a vision Abram did
  With this Spirit again commune;
Five beasts and birds he now him bid
  Prepare,—holy fire did consume.

Five sacramental types behold,
  Which it appears our God requires;
Encircle these within the fold,
  And earth will blaze with holy fire.

When this good man was ninety-nine,
  To him this Spirit once more spake,
A covenant with thee for all time,
  And to thy seed with thee I make.

Distinct from all or any race,
  His seed their children circumcise.
The Angel Christ, who did displace
  This token, with His blood despise.

Let all baptize when eight days old,
    With Abram's faith let it be done,
His name he chang'd when he was told,
    Thus Jews may Christ like yet become.

The Spirit once again appear'd
    To Abraham, when in his tent,
And, when he look'd, three men stood near;
    To these his body low he bent.

He seems to speak alone to one,
    But food prepares for all the three;
Perceive he stood till they were done,
    And Sarah hears, but does not see.

His faith is strong, but hers is weak;
    Now comes the promise of a son;
She laughs, but Abram always meek,
    Trusts, and believes all will be done.

The three move on, the Spirit stays,
    It often lingers with the pure;
When true and just are all our ways,
    His presence ever we'll secure.

The Spirit then made known to him,
    Because he rul'd his household well,
That Sodom and Gomorrah's sins,
    Sure destruction soon would tell.

Six times he to the Lord did plead,
    "The righteous pray do not destroy,"
But O, in Holy Writ we read,
    There were not ten without alloy.

Not even ten good holy men
   In those two cities could be found,
So fire and brimstone from Heaven, then
   Burnt them and all upon the ground.

The Lord, He says, went on His way,
   And Abraham to his own place.
O may we all soon see the day
   When He the earth again will grace.

'Tis true we feel His presence still,
   But then we do not see His face,
When we do all His will fulfil,
   All chang'd will be the human race.

Abraham, Isaac, and Jacob,
   Have the great God Almighty seen,
But of His name, Jehovah,
   On this earth they had not a gleam.

To Moses He did reveal
   This wonderful name with His law,
Their covenant with Him did seal,
   Under this His new name Jah.

The prophet Ezekiel saw,
   In vision, the Spirit of God;
What He spake to him was law;
   Through thorns and briars he trod.

The Spirit lifted him up
   Above worldly pleasures and cares;
Drink from this spiritual cup,
   Sav'd his soul from Satan's snares.

Jews, like the fathers of old,
   Do the great God Almighty know ;
In Christ they do not behold,
   The one whose blood will save from woe.

This God's Spirit soon will prove ;
   Once more God will to men return ;
All Evil then he will remove,
   And men will every idol burn.

His threefold essence none will doubt,
   Then all to His name, Jah, will bow,
Mankind His praises loud will shout,
   And in one Temple all will vow.

As Jesus' body knew no sin,
   God's Spirit did on him descend,
And took up his abode within,
   A voice the Spirit did attend.

When our Christ was glorified,
   On Him a cloud of light did shine,
And the voice from Heaven cried,
   " This beloved Son is mine !"

When He all His work had done,
   This cloud received Him out of sight ;
But the voice said, " He will come
   Again in that bright cloud of light !"

We should then at once prepare
   To welcome Jesus back once more ;
If we God's own armour wear,
   God will Christ to us restore.

He will then this kingdom claim,
   Righteous thoughts and deeds prevail;
Sickness, sorrow, death and pain,
   Will not us then, as now, assail.

Love to God and love to men
   Will in glorious beauty shine;
Holy actions, all will then
   Improve that holy, happy time.

None then groaning under sin,
   Will their Heavenly Father fear;
Washed and purified within,
   His voice mankind will long to hear.

THE COMMANDMENTS.

Our Father to mankind did give
   Ten commandments wise and good,
When by these commands we live,
   The tree of life will yield her food.

God in all hearts must reign supreme;
   Idols there must find no place,
No hoarded treasure seek to wean,
   Or hide us from His face.

No likeness must engross our thoughts,
   In the earth, air, sky or sea,
For God is jealous, and has taught
   That man to Him must bend the knee.

God's name we must not take in vain;
   Oaths must not our lips defile,
And when we pray to His great name,
   Nothing must our lips beguile.

To ponder on God's wondrous love,
  One day in seven we must rest,
And raise our thoughts to things above ;
  God does thus obedience test.

God has earthly parents given,
  All must honour and obey ;
Homes will be a type of heaven,
  And prolonged will be our day.

When our God and earthly parents
  Get from man what is their due,
Then the former five great talents
  Will the other five renew.

All malice will be put away.
  Anger, bitterness and strife,
Will not incite a hand to slay,
  Shortening another's life.

No selfish habits will control,
  Working out deceit and lies :
Drinking not then, inflame the soul,
  Nor poisonous love the eyes.

Then, they that stole no more will steal ;
  All our labour will be sweet,
None will envy, nor jealous feel,
  Nor any desire to cheat.

False witnesses from earth will flee ;
  Evil speaking then will cease,
And man, just like the busy bee,
  Do his daily work in peace.

Each one happy in his home
   Will not covet other's things,
But all, with one great mighty tone,
   Praise to God the Father sing.

God's ten commands will then suffice;
   Man's laws will not find a place,
For we will then have done with vice,
   And all will be wise and chaste.

A NEW PERIOD.

City of Bethlehem,
   Christ's own House of Bread,
From whence came the leaven
   That will raise the dead.

Awake from thy darkness,
   Accept the true light;
Thy houses now cheerless,
   Will all then be bright.

This desert shall rejoice,
   And bloom as the rose,
For Messiah's sweet voice
   Sin's reign soon will close.

The ransom'd will return,
   With joy on their heads,
The redeem'd will sojourn,
   As prophets have said.

With God's glory around,
   Thy mountains shall glow,
When all hallowed the ground,
   A pure vine shall grow.

In whose branches the birds
  Shall sing with one song,
And the fruit of Christ's words
  Be seen in the throng.

No more shall the curse
  God's children oppress,
Neither mourner nor hearse
  Their hearts shall distress.

Awake, then, this New-Year,
  Arouse thee from sleep;
Angel voices I hear,
  Their vigils they keep.

Hark! the Archangel's voice
  Proclaims He is come,
The righteous rejoice,
  A crown they have won.

Earth's sweet Sabbath rest.
  Long life will restore;
Christ again as man's guest,
  Will reign evermore.

AN APPEAL TO
THE WORLD IN GENERAL.
The Citizens of the Dominion in Particular.

Many Poems like these
  Are ready to print.
The Saints will God please,
  If, after this hint,

They give freely their gold ;
　　Such truths to display,
God will blessings untold
　　Shower down day by day.

" The Christian's Wedding Ring,"
　　The name it will bear ;
For the Saviour our King,
　　It bids earth prepare.

It has search'd far and wide,
　　Its gilding to find,
But all lay it aside
　　As too good to bind.

" Write a novel or story,
　　That will sell," they say ;
Of our future glory,
　　" O no ! that won't pay."

For the body most men
　　Their energies spend,
But their souls now and then
　　Would like them to lend

A fair share of the wealth
　　It helps to provide,
For alas ! with great stealth,
　　Its wants are supplied.

Now, in this age of strikes,
　　Before it rebels,
Let this work see the light,
　　It evil dispels.

God's own word is the mine
  Producing this ore ;
With Christ's Spirit Divine
  All thus may explore.

And produce finer gold,
  New beauties display,
Which will never grow old,
  Nor ever decay.

NAPOLEON'S DEATH.

Another of the son's of men,
  Who did earth's glories taste,
The Emperor Napoleon,
  Death stole away in haste.

'Midst scenes of woe, and joy, and mirth,
  His three-score years and five
Have swiftly sped away on earth,
  No longer will he strive

An earthly Empire here to guide,
  Or countrymen control ;
The space that he and them divide,
  Angels alone patrol.

The prize for which he strove—he won,
  While in his prime—and lost,
Before his life on earth was done.
  Was it worth the cost ?

Ambition, his besetting sin,
  Caus'd him to wage a war ;
Amidst its roar and deaf'ning din,
  He was the one lost star.

These worldly crowns at best are nought,
    They yield no lasting joy;
When the battle of life is fought,
    Vain is the glittering toy.

But virtue's crown will never fade,
    Nor will it dim with age,
For each one such a crown is made,
    Strive for it and be sage.

THE FOUR PERIODS OF THE WORLD.

Four Periods the world has seen,
    God's wonders each has shown;
First mighty waters tried to wean
    Man from his gods of stone.

The Patriarchal then begun,
    Some good men then did shine;
With might great Pharoah was undone,
    And Israel mov'd in line.

The Levitical then burst forth,
    Its rays from Sinai came;
Gold images of greater worth
    Man worshipped all the same.

This period clos'd with awful death
    Of Christ, the Son of God;
Man worships still his gods of earth,
    And bends not to the rod.

This great High Priest from death did rise,
    He taught men holy ways;
His body our great sacrifice,
    The dawn of brighter days.

This Period draws near its close,
   Evil has had its day;
God soon with goodness will descend,
   Reanimate the clay.

Our spirits then will daily grow
   More lovely, more divine;
New graces then the soul will show,
   And round the body twine.

THE DYING YEAR OF 1872.

The dying of another year
Brings round some memories dear,
Of many joys that now are dead,
Happy days which all have fled.

But still hope welcomes to our hearts,
New year with its open chart;
And if new lines we try to trace,
Peace and joy will fill each face.

The year from us does quickly hide;
One by one the minutes slide.
Has it left golden threads behind?
All our future lives to bind.

Or will its deeds, the coming year,
Cause us many a groan and tear?
Have we been honest, just and true,
Given God what is His due?

Have we smiled sweetly in our homes,
Mounted high on virtue's throne,
Been kind to all within our reach,
Acted well what Christ did teach?

These are the steps the Saints have trod,
Gems like these their feet have shod;
May we, untarnished, like them, see
The Reign of Christ in seventy-three.

Wishing you all a Happy New Year,
Light from God our hearts to cheer,
Love to cement the Christian Ring,
Altogether we will sing,
Alleluia.

THE

SERPENT

SATAN

FALSE PROPHET

THE TRINITY OF EVIL.

THE EVIL SPIRIT.

The Evil Spirit is the theme
   I now before you set in verse;
I wish to draw aside the screen,
   And all his ways and works rehearse.

A Trinity of Evil see,
Now surrounding land and sea;
St. John three unclean spirits saw
Coming from the dragon's jaw.

Like frogs, he says, they leapt about,
Croaking all their evil out;
Working miracles, man to cleave,
Just as he did first with Eve.

What a deceiver he has been,
   This Prince of the pow'r of the air;
His only object, aim and scheme,
   That man should all his ruin share.

Like light'ning he from Heaven fell,
   Knowing he never could return;
But would be closely shut in Hell,
   For endless ages to sojourn.

While man, if he obey'd God's laws,
   He saw would fill his vacant place,
And revel in all those great joys,
   He lost when he did Heav'n disgrace.

This must have fill'd his wicked heart
    With envy, jealousy and hate,
And led him on to play the part
    Which lur'd our parents to their fate.

Then, as a serpent, he appears
    To a gentle trusting woman,
Filling her mind with doubts and fears,
    As he leads her through the garden.

" If that fine beauteous fruit you eat,
    " God will not surely make you die ;
" As gods you will then take your seat,
    " And good from evil with your eye

" Well opened, you will discern."
    Instead of which, how many sin
On, day by day, with no concern,
    For he has made all dark within ;

And death, the dreadful curse of man
    And beast, for near six thousand years
The whole of this our earth doth span ;
    While Satan walks around and leers,

Tempting each creature with his fruit,
    Which all too eagerly do taste ;
His poison made each one to suit,
    And all his energies to waste.

Job tells us of a certain day,
    When many of our God's own sons,
Mov'd by a holy, heavenly ray,
    Together to the Lord did come.

Among them Satan finds his way,
    And to the Lord himself did talk.
" My servant Job, the Lord did say,
    " In true and upright paths doth walk."

But Satan cunningly replies:
  "An hedge about him thou hast made;
"The reason why he me defies,
  Thy blessings have him firmly staid."

Pow'r to Satan the Lord then gave,
  His servant Job to try and tempt;
Strong faith from Satan's wiles did save—
  His love to God they did cement.

As Joshua the High Priest stands
  Before the Angel of the Lord,
Satan resists at his right hand,
  But disappears at Angel's word.

The filthy garments he had worn
  Were then from Joshua taken;
His head a mitre did adorn,
  When Satan had him forsaken.

David by Satan was provok'd
  To number up Israel's hosts,
By which God's anger he invok'd
  And sev'nty thousand men he lost.

Thus David, Joshua and Job,
  Have sin and Satan seen and known;
All Adam's children on this globe,
  Have been by Satan made to groan.

Nothing but the Saviour's prayer
Sav'd Simon Peter from his lair;
Three times he made him tell a lie,
For which he afterwards did sigh.

Jude says, the Devil did dispute,
And the Archangel did refute;
Moses, for whom he did contend,
This Angel Michael did defend.

But Christ has bruis'd the Serpent's head,
    And curb'd his great and wondrous power;
When he returns to wake the dead,
    His Angel chains him in that hour.

LUKE XIII. 32.

When Christ did on this earth appear,
    The Devil first as man was seen;
To tempt us he is always near—
    Various is his shape and mien.

He dar'd our Lord himself to tempt;
    But foil'd, he plung'd with rage in men;
And women were not then exempt—
    From Magdalene Christ cast out seven.

See how those devils knew our Lord,
    And trembled when they saw His face;
They flew when He but spake the word—
    The swine into the lake did chase.

The Devil still does men possess,
    When evil passions do enthral;
His idols seem to have a zest
    And pow'r to make men hear his call.

Slyly he flatters and deceives,
    Allures each one with some device;
Inflates with pride or love of ease—
    With golden rays he does entice.

Men blindly nibble at his fruit,
    Although its poison well they know
His snares are laid each one to suit,
    Causing his evil seed to grow.

To the twelve Christ gave the power
    To check the growth of sin in man;
From His throne He now does shower
    Grace on the means of his great plan,

Which fills his sacraments with fire;
    Gives strength to bruise the tempter's arts;
Preserves from Satan's rage and ire,
    Rendering harmless all his darts.

Christ alone can extract the root
    And take the sting of death away;
When man does heed his Maker's suit,
    Christ will proclaim eternal day.

THE TEMPTER'S ARTS.

How grievous is the love of gain,
When it does men's souls enchain;
Cheating and grasping all they can,
Then the daily hourly plan.

To gain a little bit of land,
Many will soul and body strand;
Pass restless days and sleepless nights,
Scheming plots for other's rights.

They will cause you both pain and toil,
If their arts you try to foil;
Against them you cannot succeed,
Unless God does intercede.

One with another will combine,
To work out their dark design;
In a great circle they will join
What they covet to purloin.

To be thought rich in gold and land,
They will rob you underhand;
Thus many a noble life is lost,
And with evil passions tost.

Self, the sole object of each thought,
When their labour comes to nought:
The things of sight their value lose,
Too late virtue's paths to choose.

Despair drives on to darker deeds—
Fruit of all their evil seeds—
Worries the mind, wears flesh away,
Clothes with sorrow and decay.

2ND PART.

The love of gold absorbs all else,
Men seem to live to gather pence;
Never content, their constant aim,
Is gold and silver heaps to gain.

Some make it in an honest way,
With steady aim from day to day;
They gather coin, build mansions great,
That they may live in grand estate.

Some with sharp tricks and cheating ways,
Their friends and foes alike betray;
Grow very rich, and very proud,
And drive their horses with the crowd.

Some save and scrape, and live by stealth,
That men may bow to their great wealth;
These ends attained, they pass away,
Are cut down as the new mown hay.

Does it seem wisdom thus to live,
And all our energies to give;
To gather what we cannot keep,
And sow where we so little reap?

Gold is a useful thing, 'tis true;
All have a right to get their due;
But if for it our minds we strain,
Then slyly Satan twines his chain;

Making us selfish, mean and vain,
The glory of this world our aim;
The heart grows cold, the eye grows dim,
All from this great and grievous sin.

Even the monkey has more sense,
He prefers nuts to any pence;
Darwin's theory must be wrong,
For man's improving is his song.

SABBATH BREAKING.

Am I robbing God or not,
   If I use the Sabbath day
To work out my worldly plots,
   Or to mingle with the gay?

Six days work, one day of rest,
   Is our Maker's own command;
Man seems to think it's a jest,
   And heeds not this wise demand.

Those we love, we try to please,
   Gladly we devote to them
All our thoughts, our time, our ease,
   Giving all to sinful men;

While we steal our Maker's hours,
    Just to take a little sail;
To stroll in beauty's bowers,
    Or write letters for the mail.

Some read novels all the day,
    Visit all their friends around;
Gather Idols made of clay,
    With a false and hollow sound.

Softly down these paths men tread,
    On the way to greater crimes;
Prisoners by Satan led,
    Willing captives to his wiles.

Always craving something new,
    Peace of mind they never know;
Seldom any good pursue,
    And God's blessings from them throw.

THE SIN OF DRINKING.

Serpents of every kind are seen,
    Winding through the forest glade;
In search of prey their eyes do gleam,
    Finding victims in its shade.

The Serpent lures with magic eye—
    Courage flies beneath his gaze;
The victim tries in vain to fly,
    Fascinated, there it stays.

Poison and death from him have sprung,
    And in ev'ry mouth is found;
Saliva to our lips has clung—
    Death our bodies does surround.

With light'ning dash the creature springs,
    And at once does it enfold;
Coils round and round; and to it clings,
    Till its jaws its body hold.

When Eve did with the Serpent talk,
    Subtle he was, it is said;
But then he on his feet did walk;
    Now, all creatures do him dread.

Our very blessings made a curse
    That which should have cheered the heart,
Causing constant craving thirst—
    Sowing vice of ev'ry sort.

Drink is the greatest curse of sin,
    Few the habit can control;
It makes all black and dark within—
    Ruins body, mind and soul.

It is many a household's foe,
    Wearing flesh and health away;
Dragging souls down to endless woe;
    Hiding from them Christ our stay.

Just like a little pebble thrown
    In water, quiet and calm,
It ruffles and disturbs this stone,
    All the circle that it can.

One seldom hears of any crime,
    Where drink has not play'd its part;
It seems to be the evil mine,
    With veins pointing to the heart.

But Jesus, who was all Divine,
    New life offers to those veins;
Drink in faith His love in wine,
    And thus shake off Satan's chains.

FLIRTING.

Flirting is a fearful thing,
   Leads to much sorrow and shame;
Hearts it does with sorrow wring,
   It should some attention claim.

Little children now we see,
   Whose hearts should be pure indeed,
Looking all around with glee,
   For a little of this weed,

Which, when planted, grows apace,
   Spoils that sweet and lovely bloom,
Which should shine on each young face,
   Many virtues does entomb.

Then when these young people wed,
   Flirting ways they cannot change;
They continue, without dread,
   And each other's hearts estrange.

Then the little daily strife
   Wears till it creates a sore;
Tarnishing the joys of life,
   Gnawing out love's very core.

There can be no sadder sight
   Than a home with hearts grown cold;
Without love, its beacon light,
   Serpents poison and enfold.

Just as one did Mother Eve,
   With a little gentle sting;
Each the other does deceive,
   And to utter ruin bring.

THE SIN OF LYING.

The devil's children must tell lies,
He always has a liar been
To speak the truth, they never try
He always from it tries to wean.

First disobey then tell a lie,
If you my wages wish to gain,
God surely will not make you die
He must have whisper'd unto Cain.

It does seem strange when Abel died,
That fear of man should fill Cain's mind
That with a lie he thought to hide
A deed of such a dreadful kind.

From the great God whose truth he saw
In his dead brother's form of clay,
Why was he not o'erwhelm'd with awe
Instead of fear that man would slay.

The devil held him in his grasp,
And gently from his God withdrew,
He slowly fasten'd on the mask
That hid from him the wise and true.

This is the way he marches round,
Filling the earth with lying seed,
And trying to maintain his ground
By urging men to wicked deeds.

CHURCH MUSIC.

Is it true that notes of praise
In our churches discords raise;
Evil does in there intrude,
Even there he tries to brood

Why should we to Satan yield ?
Let us drive him from the field ;
Sift and see though he defies
And poor human nature tries.

Some no organ will allow,—
To this prejudice they bow ;
Some will not stand up to sing,—
Never think of such a thing.

Young boy singers clad in white
Are to some a great delight.
Ladies some call to their aid,
But then they must *now* be paid.

Some make music the one thing,
People flock to hear them sing ;
Finish up with some new lay,
Just to make the people stay.

Organs are of ancient date,
For in man's primeval state
Harp and organ we are told,
Jubal could himself take hold.

And in Chronicles we read
When King David saw the need
For the Ark to pitch a tent,
He for Priests and Levites sent.

That they might prepare to sing,
Praises to our God and King ;
They did Chenaniah choose,
Because he among the Jews

Was most skilful in the song,
And could best instruct the throng ;
David dress'd in linen white,
Singers, Levites all in sight.

Priests did all their trumpets blow,
And the Word doth further show
They play'd cornets, cymbals, harps,
Shouting forth with all their hearts;

And in Nehemiah's day
Priests and Levites met to pray,
With singers, instruments and all,
Who upon the Lord did call.

Thus it seems that Jewish times
Brought forth more united chimes;
When to Christ Jews bend the knee,
Christians will their errors see.

THE TEMPTER'S FRIENDS.

Come, friends, the Summer is coming on fast,
The Winter is now very nearly past;
Let us pitch our tents, and arrange our ways,
Where there are no Holy Sabbath days.

Lachine, they say, is a very nice place,
Then to it we all must most surely haste;
The rich and the poor are gathering there,
So it is plain we have no time to spare.

Our company must be very select,
Satan, our guide, we'll agree to elect;
The seventh day in his amusements spend,
He will give us fun, and some money lend.

We will moor our boats on Saturday night,
And start in the morning, just at day-light;
It would be just as well to get away
When people are looking the other way;

For when all the Church bells begin to ring;
And these good Christians begin to sing,
We'll feel our bodies are stealing the rest,
Our souls would enjoy with relish and zest.

But now 'tis too late our ways to change,
Our habits are form'd, our plans arranged;
Our spiritual eyes are firmly sealed,
Our future Satan has well concealed.

THE LAST BATTLE.

Lucifer, who from Heaven fell,
And whose domain is now call'd Hell,
Would gladly wander over earth
And gather angels for his hearth.

Lucifer knows his time is short,
Thus he is luring every sort;
Some with gold, and some with wine,
Some he draws with a steady line.

Lucifer, when he makes men sin,
Whispers, "it is but a little thing;
"Taste and try it, it is really sweet;"
He soon persuades, and mankind eat.

Lucifer is cunning and sly;
He never works, but he must lie;
His greatest card, a pile of gold,
Draws foolish souls into his hold.

Lucifer's door is near at hand;
Goodness will drive him from this land;
Then death, our enemy, will flee,
And man will purely happy be.

THE KINGDOM.

The question is on earth who reigns,
Who is it holds man's heart in chains,
Who tempts us with his golden rays,
And tries to make us passion's slaves.

Look at the young and lovely babe,
Perfect by his Creator made.
How soon will anger spoil that face,
And rob it of its sweetest grace.

Before it speaks it disobeys,
And seems to crave for evil ways.
The tongue soon learns to tell a lie,
For which 'tis hard to make it sigh.

If Christ had not put on a curb,
Nothing would evil still disturb,
His good and noble early life
Has this kingdom fill'd with strife.

He told us that he brought a sword
That would us through sins' river ford,
And with the sword, Faith's golden chain
This dreadful battle to maintain.

As long as man this conflict fights
Death will put him out of sight,
The hour of temptations come,
The voice will soon proclaim 'tis done.

The time of peace is drawing near,
Then we will nothing have to fear,
The former things will pass away,
And we will Christ all homage pay.

THE VICTORY.

Evil now sits in glory great,
Spreading round his tempting bait;
Luring us with the things of sight,
To the realms of endless night.

Two spirits now for us contend,
And our wills' behests attend;
One will with holiness array,
The other leads our steps astray.

The good must trust, and watch and wait;
Their reward anticipate;
For while this world is rul'd by sin,
They their glory cannot win.

Christ comes again with a reprieve,
When the Jews in him believe;
Then as the King of David's line,
He will open out their mine.

Then earth will be Heaven below,
Time no longer will us mow;
Many purified then will be,
And made white that all shall see.

All hallowed then our Father's name,
Christ will this his Kingdom claim;
His will on earth will then be done
As in Heaven it is sung.

He will give us our daily Bread,
And the Blood which he has shed
Will furnish food for soul and mind
Of the best and rarest kind.

Our trespasses God will forgive,
And will give us strength to live,
As Christ did walk so good and kind,
To each other's faults quite blind.

Temptations then will not assail;
For our sight will pierce the vail
Of that dark desolated land,
Where evil dwells on ev'ry hand.

The wicked there will all have fled,
Captive then by Satan led;
Banished for ever from the sight
Of God's presence pure and bright.

Satan having claimed his own,
And withdrawn them to his home;
In glory on the mercy seat,
God will his good subjects meet.

With might and power then will shine
The wisdom of our God Divine;
Mankind will then his name adore,
Pray and praise him evermore.

DEATH.

Death now places his icy hand
On ev'ry creature in the land,
As people walk along the street,
Hearse or mourner they're sure to meet.

Why is it so? My spirit asks,
The young, the old must wear his mark,
Must drive along the dusty street,
And furnish to the worms his meat.

Nor cloister'd cell nor stately hall,
But what must answer to his call
The rich, the poor, the fool, the wise
Go to the grave yard, there he lies.

What is the reason, angel hear
Why must I part with all that's dear.
Why must I leave this lovely earth,
And make an end of all my mirth.

The angel whisper'd in my ear,
Man's idols make death tarry here,
Unite with faith and Christian love,
And soon will come the Holy Dove.

Who when he comes will clear the way,
Illumine all things with his ray,
Restore to us the life we lost,
And make us like, the Heav'nly Host.

To His Most Illustrious Majesty,

THE GRAND SEIGNEUR AND SULTAN

OF THE OTTOMAN EMPIRE:

In the year 1870, I offered you my congratulations on the successful manner which you accomplished the opening of the Canal, which gives direct communication from the Mediterranean to the Red Sea; and the visit of the Empress of France, at that time in all her glory, seems to have been the commencement of direct intercourse between Turks and Christians, preparing the way for the return of the Jews to Jerusalem—which event appears to me to be very near at hand.

Since then, the Empress has been bereft of her husband and driven from the country where she reigned supreme—teaching us that we live in a time of wonderful changes. Indeed, the signs of the times are such as to make all men prepare for the Second coming of the Lord; and, if He is indeed coming with ten thousand of His Saints, as prophesied by Enoch, the seventh from Adam, all should use their talents to bring the world to one united Faith and Practice. You and I agree in the fact that all the world is descended from Noah, and the first good man who is mentioned after the Flood is Abraham, from whom both you and I descend,—for he had two sons, Isaac and Ishmael, both circumcised after the law, (the Jews are the descendants of Isaac, the Mahomedans of Ishmael). Christ was descended in a direct line from Isaac, and we are baptised and by that means made his children, by adoption.

Now Abraham believed that a Sacrifice of Blood was needed, and for that faith the Lord himself appeared to him twice and promised him that, "*In thee* shall *all* the families of the earth be blessed, (Genesis xii., 3,) "All the nations of the earth shall be blessed *in him*," (Genesis xviii., 18,) "and in *thy seed* shall *all* the nations of the earth be blessed, (Genesis xxii., 18.) If Christ, then, in whom we believe, was the Lord who appeared to our Father Abraham three different times, He must have been the child of promise, of whom Isaac was the Type.

Our natural birth does not make us Christians. We may be born of Christian parents, in a Christian land; but, unless baptised of water and of the Spirit, we are neither of the nation or family of Christ, nor is the seed of the Holy Spirit sown in our hearts. Christ, then, in whom we believe, and whose children we are made by baptism, was circumcised and fulfilled the law in every particular. Without the Divine nature of God he could not have done this, for human nature, since the fall, has been unable to do anything perfectly. Christ suffered death, in order that every creature that breathed the breath of life might be set free from the bondage of sin, and so fitted to appear before God, the Maker of the world.

Thus, we see that Abraham believed in Christ before He (Christ) came into the world; we have the testimony of living witnesses who saw Him, and the daily fulfilment of Prophecies which he could not have understood; for as God divided the Red Sea on former days to allow the Jews to pass through on dry land, so now he has allowed you to make a passage through the Red Sea to the Holy Land, the place in which the Prophet Joel, hundreds of years ago, prophesied the descent of the Holy Spirit, and where Micah says, (chap. iv., 6, 7,) all the nations of the earth will come to a knowledge of the truth.

"The Rabbins say, that when the lot was taken, a scarlet fillet was bound on the Scape Goat's head, and after the High Priest had confessed his and the people's sins over it, the fillet became white; this miracle ceased, according to them, forty years before the destruction of Jerusalem, that is, exactly when Jesus Christ was crucified."

Now, it may be that our blood was white before the Evil Spirit's poison entered our veins, and this miracle may have been intended to show that God will purify and make white again the blood of those who spiritually partake of those Sacraments that God has provided for the soul's nourishment. We know that Christ shed his blood drop by drop to make atonement for the sins of the whole world, not for a few Christians or a few Jews,—not for one sect or one church,—but for the sins of the whole world, to satisfy Divine Justice and Mercy; and when mankind begins to realize this fact, the sole object of their lives will be to become pure, Holy and Christ-like, and to make this earth a Heaven below.

But the Soul, like the body, must use the Blood to make it pure, in the same way as the body requires to use water to make it clean. Nothing but the *use* of water can keep the body in health; nothing but the *use* of Christ's Blood can cleanse and purify the soul.

There are at present in the world numberless sects, but only four religions: Jews, Mahomedans, and Christians, who worship the one holy and true God, and Heathens who worship Idols of wood or stone or false Gods; all four of which seem represented by Jewish offerings, which were first the offering of the herds of the flock, a shadow of the Jewish Faith which, until Christ came, always slew a lamb for their Passover. The offering of the first fruits, which was Cain's offering, rejected of God, typifying the Mahomedan. The Peace offering, which was a type of Christ himself; for St. Paul, in Ephesians ii., 14, says: "Christ is our Peace, he has broken down the wall of sin that hid us from God. And the offering of the sin of ignorance, which represents the Heathen, who surely worship, in ignorance, Idols of wood and stone. If this is the case, how truly did St. Paul say in Hebrews x., 1: "The Law having a shadow of good things to come and not the very image of those things, can never, with those sacrifices which they offered year by year continually, make the comers thereunto perfect."

Before addressing you, I have devoted myself to the study of the Prophet Mahomet and the English version of the Koran. The Prophet appears before me with a tall and commanding figure, strong in mind, earnest in purpose, and sincere in what he professed and wrote, with great reverence for the Almighty God, but wanting in the knowledge of God's threefold Essence as manifested in the person of Jesus Christ and the Holy Spirit. Although I find in the Koran many proofs which have helped to strengthen my faith in Christianity, a few of which I will quote: Take page 13 of 2nd Book, "The Angel Gabriel is said to have caused the Koran to descend on his heart;" now it is the Holy Spirit of God alone that puts every good thought in our hearts; the page 36 of 3rd Book says: "O Lord, thou shalt gather mankind together unto a day of resurrection: there is no doubt of it, for God will not be contrary to his promise." Now, in Revelations chap. i., 7, it says: "Behold, He cometh with clouds, and every eye shall see Him, and they also which pierced Him, and all kindreds of the earth shall wail because of Him."

Then page 40, 41 speaks of "God," "the Angel," and the "Word," the three distinct offices of Father, Son and Spirit. Then chapter 19, page 251, calls Jesus the Son of Mary, "the Word of Truth," proving plainly Christ's divine and human nature. It is a great mystery and hard to understand; but the Devil is a mystery, and his temptations quite beyond our comprehension, and often so veiled that we scarcely see them till we have felt their sting; one thing is certain, it is his chief object to keep all mankind from knowing God as a God of infinite Love, so great that He condescended to live on earth, with man, and to die for man, so that God's justice might be satisfied. If God, who made the world and all mankind, breathed into man a spirit which shall *never die*, could He not breathe into Christ's human body a Spirit which should never sin. Then that body, not having been polluted by sin, would be an Atonement for all the world, provided they had faith strong enough to believe that Divine wrath was satisfied; but we must have a living Faith, not a trust in Fate or Islem.

The beautiful plates, which appeared in the London papers, of the splendid ceremony which attended the opening of the Canal, on that memorable 17th November, 1870, afforded their readers much pleasure; but the sublime idea of having the work blessed by all religions was the dawn of a new period — and all those vessels, with their various flags, sailing in one direction, under one guide, a foreshadowing of the time when all will sail under the Banner of the Cross, with one King, even CHRIST.

Then those canopies and gorgeous arrangements will again draw together the Jew with the Crescent, beneath the Cross — around which will twine that living vine, whose fruit will strengthen and renew all that eat and drink, in faith, of that spiritual food, which, though now lost to our natural sight, through sin, is still within the reach of the faithful.

The writer hopes that these remarks will induce the Turks to search the Scriptures, and see who was the true Prophet, Christ or Mahomet. The latter, in his life, had many more followers than Christ; but after the lapse of so many years, which has been the greatest benefit to mankind — Mahommadism, which was established at the point of the sword, or the Christian one, which will only shine forth in all its beauty when our swords are firmly fastened in their sheaths ? That you, when Christ returns to reign for a thousand years, may have your name written in the Book of Life, is the sincere wish of the writer, who is a Christian Lady, of the first city of the first Dominion in the world.—(Micah iv., 8.)

THE CHRISTIAN'S FAITH.

O ! Turkish maidens fair and bright,
Bring all your Crescents to the light ;
Try Mahomet's laws by Christ's commands,
And see with whom the glory stands.

The Koran's page in this our day,
Transmits a secondary ray ;
Its gems all borrow'd seem to be,
From God's word sent to you and me.

When Mahomet wrote that wondrous work,
Which chang'd the Heathen to a Turk,
The word of God was then fulfill'd,
And Abram's seed with truth instill'd.

But now God's spirit comes with pow'r ;
Make ready friends for that great hour,
When pain and sorrow, sickness, woe,
And all man's troubles here below

Will from this earth be swept away—
God will restore eternal day—
And diamonds, crowns and precious stones,
Will shine on those who fill the thrones.

THE CHRISTIAN'S LOVE.

Jewish maidens, far and near,
Come to God's messenger and hear
The wondrous tale the word reveals,
Of He who all our sorrow heals.

'Tis true, He died by Jewish bands ;
But Christians too have pierc'd his hands ;
Drawn blood and water from his side ;
Inflicted pangs of human pride.

The sacrifice that He has made;
The thorns that on his brow were laid;
Will draw sin's poison from our veins,
And cleanse our souls from all sin's stains.

O! let me lift the veil that hides
The Saviour's virtues from your eyes.
O! let me teach you that you must,
Like Him, be perfect, pure and just.

At once begin your lamps to trim,
With holy fire and grace within;
Come quickly to the marriage feast
Of Jewish, Turkish, Christian Priest.

THE CHRISTIAN'S CROSS.

For nearly nineteen hundred years
Christians have been shedding tears;
Struggling, striving, meekly bearing
Scorns and slights; yes, ever wearing

Satan's grievous heavy crosses,
And trying to maintain the loss
Of the One who came to teach them
How to live like Christian men.

For forty long and weary days,
The Saviour, with evil ways
The Tempter tried to overcome,
But there he found himself undone.

He calmly yielded up his life,
Pierc'd to the heart with all the strife;
He hasten'd to the spirit land—
Such love is hard to understand.

Again He trod this sinful ground,
And shed His glory all around,
For forty days, obedient, kind,
All virtue's graces left behind.

He rose above us out of sight,
But still he cheers our souls with light;
The spark that lit the Heav'nly flame
Will forever our souls sustain.

Soon He will come in regal state,
With an array of angels great;
No crosses then for us to bear—
Our crowns will meet us in the air.

Prepare then, all the bridegrooms near;
Ten thousand saints will see and hear;
The righteous then will hardly stand—
The wicked fall on every hand.

On hearing a sermon on the 63rd Isaiah, 3rd verse:
"I HAVE TRODDEN THE WINEPRESS ALONE."

Christ has trodden alone
The wine press, to atone;
He bore the burden of sin,
And drew from it the sting.

His soul such sorrow knew,
That from its lips it drew;
"This cup, Father, pass away,
"Thy will to do, I pray."

In drops he sweat his blood
To stop the fatal flood;
The agony was great,
Our race to reinstate.

Come then to this pure vine,
And drink his blood in wine;
In bread His body take,
And sin will us forsake.

Our faith will then defeat
The tempter's arts we meet;
The mercy seat will shine
Again with light divine.

The Jews, in days of yore,
The Temple purg'd with gore;
Then birds and beasts supplied
The blood that justified.

Two goats the High Priest brought;
And as he had been taught,
He lots for them did cast,
That one he might make fast,

A sin offering to make,
That God would not forsake;
The other he cast away,
For Jewish sins to pay.

A scarlet fillet bound
The scape goat's head around;
To white its color chang'd,
Till virtue Christ maintain'd

Now even Rabbins say,
This miracle that they
So long beheld did cease,
When death did Christ release.

If once the blood was white,
And men both pure and bright,
When sin we learn to shun,
Again, as then, will run

The pure blood in our veins;
Christ then will take the reins,
And fill with joy our hearts,
For Satan then departs.

When Faith and Works embrace,
And all our actions grace;
Then look! behold the sign
Of the Millenium, Time.

All Idols forsaken,
New life will awaken;
Both the body and soul
Christ will cleanse and make whole;

For His woes paid the cost,
And the joys Adam lost
To this earth will return,
When God's truth we all learn.

THE WRECK OF THE ATLANTIC,

On Mars Island, 1st April, 1873.

A ship well built as man can boast,
Has just founder'd on the coast
Of a rocky Island,—Mars by name,
Sad the nature of its fame.

Ten days had hardly pass'd away
Since with hearts both light and gay,
Almost a thousand souls embark'd
In this ship, this treach'rous ark.

When all on board are wrap't in sleep,
But the watch, who vigils keep;
Just three o'clock, "All's well," they shout,
"Hark! breakers ahead! look out!"

The vessel strikes against a rock,
And receives a fatal shock;
The boilers burst, she over heels,
To the raging water yields.

Which draws her down beneath the wave,
Hundreds find a watery grave;
Both men and women, girls and boys,
Hush'd are all their fears and joys.

These left their friends no parting word,
One loud shriek alone was heard;
No Priest could make them then confess,
No religion them redress.

Alone their spirits all did soar,
To that unknown distant shore;
Some to return with glory great,
Some to find the truth too late.

Some were sav'd by means of rope,
When almost bereft of hope;
One by *Ancients* Priestly hand
Was in safety brought to land.

This teaches us not to despair,
But to lift our hearts in prayer;
To use the means God has ordain'd,
And then all will be regained.

THE ST. LAWRENCE,

As she appeared on the 19*th April*, 1873.

River St. Lawrence in a shroud,
    Is sleeping peacefully
Around her banks behold a crowd,
    Awaiting anxiously.

To see her burst those icy bands,
    They very fearfully
Cast their eyes on all low lands
    While praying fervently.

That she will not their ground o'erflow
    But gently, peacefully,
They wish her to awake and show
    Quiet and gratefully.

That for her blessed time of rest,
    Which they bore patiently,
She will assume her very best,
    Retiring modestly.

One might suggest a melting mood,
    So that she carefully
Should change her death like attitude,
    And come out joyously.

With dress of beaut'ous wavy blue,
    Then all will lovingly
Pay her the homage that is due,
    By sailing joyously.

And then with hearts both light and gay,
    All will most thankfully
Enjoy the summer holiday,
    Hailing her cheerfully.

All working with labour and skill
    Quite industriously,
Tracing out the Creator's will,
    Yes, harmoniously.

A PRAYER.

Thy work is waiting, Father dear,
For means to send it forth,
O, send me some kind friend to cheer;
One that will see its worth.

Some say, poor thing, how very sad,
To see such waste of time,
Such writing soon will make you *mad;*
Don't write another line.

Do help the work I gently plead
Its precepts all are true;
I have not any time to read,
So 'tis in vain to sue.

Do be advised another says,
A cent you'll never make
For good books no one ever pays,
So no more trouble take.

Reform the world, another cries,
All very fine to talk,
Man now has grown so very wise,
In sin he likes to walk.

Still hope is lurking in my breast,
Some saint, I think, I'll find,
To say, O what a welcome guest,
I'll store it in my mind.

Its precepts all are good and true,
Great and grand its aims,
Reject them not because they're new,
And teach one self to tame.

Subdue one self, how great the thought,
Keep each passion down,
How Christ-like, just what Jesus taught,
No longer he will frown.

Once more I urge its claims, pray help
To spread its praise around,
I always said, and always felt
God's work in it resounds.

For no one could alone have trac'd
A book of such a kind,
Its pages with such beauties grac'd,
As you in it will find.

And though each person may have read
Its contents oft before,
Some soul may in it find the thread,
One temple to restore.

TRUTH.

A stripling in the search of truth
    To foreign lands did wend his way,
In musty books this charming youth
    Thought he could find truth's holy ray

Of course no trace of truth he found,
    So thought that in his head would place
Ancient learning most profound,
    Sweeten'd with pleasure to his taste.

The folly pleas'd his body well,
    The learning fill'd his mind with pride;
His spirit well he could not tell,
    Why he its food did always hide.

Years pass'd, and as he older grew,
    Some change he thought it well to see;
A little gold would make things new,
    So daily work it then must be.

His idol gold at once became,
    All search for truth he set aside;
His heart he set on earthly gain,
    And Satan soon became his guide.

Some years in piling gold he pass'd,
    But there all trace of truth he lost;
Now heaps of gold he has amass'd,
    But Oh! to him how great the cost.

When he reach'd the palace of truth,
    No passport had he in his mind,
The angel asked him why in youth
    He had not gathered of this kind?

He said that truth was once his aim,
   But all is false and hollow here;
The angel did to him exclaim,
   Did not Christ teach you how to steer.

Had you your bible daily sought
   For grace and strength to overcome
You would have learnt and others taught
   How this glittering gem is won.

The man then paus'd quite sad, to think
   He never there had thought to look,
For joys to fill that missing link,
   The way of truth in God's own book.

A PRAYER.

O teach me, teach me, Lord, I pray,
How I can thy work array,
That it may draw the Jew to thee,
At thy cross to bend the knee.

To make them feel thou hast been here,
All our hearts with love to cheer;
To teach them that thy pow'r so great
Chose to come in low estate.

The evil one so well ensnares,
Hearts so fills with earthly cares,
That works like mine they do not prize,
For it so the spirit tries.

But, if God's truth it does contain,
He my efforts will sustain,
And, in spite of all man's pride,
Will disperse it far and wide.

Pray, Esau's sons, come chaff the wheat!
Draw Christ from his heavenly seat!
Search with me this precious mine,
And you will with glory shine.

Come humbly to the throne of grace,
Worship him, who fills all space,
With faith and love, a small return
Which Christ left his throne to earn.

Pride is the Evil One's delight—
For it hides God from our sight;
Like children, try to learn and trust
That God's plan is wise and just.

The veil must rise from off your eyes,
Before Jesus you can prize;
And earth can never heaven become
Till your homage Christ has won.

Death draws us, now, with noiseless tread;
Generations he has led
Through his great valley, dark and lone,
Breaking up man's earthly home.

Gloom and darkness, sorrow and woe,
Are found where his scythe doeh mow;
He persecutes the human race—
Each in turn he does embrace.

The aged parent, child, and slave,
All descend into the grave;
It matters little what your creed,
Each in turn that way proceed.

Then let me urge, yes, beg, entreat,
That my work you soon will greet
With a generous, welcome look,
Searching well through all the book.

Then making trial of its truth,
By imparting it to youth;
So that the glory it portrays
May be brought within our gaze.

SECOND PART.

Our lives are all a mystery,
   From our childhood to old age;
Each one would make a history,
   And fill full many a page.

A warfare rages all through life,
   Man's heart, the great prize, to gain,
'Tis evil causes all the strife,
   And with sin our souls does chain.

God sends good angels us to guide,
   Holy seed within to plant;
The Devil watches, makes us slide,
   And with evil does enchant.

King David was both pure and good,
   When God's house he thought to build;
He tasted of the tempter's food,
   And with sin his soul he fill'd.

When Nathan, who the Lord did send
   His servant to reprimand,
Convinced him he must amend,
   And obey his God's command.

He shewed him how life's journey all
   With great blessings God had crown'd
Whenever he on him had call'd
   His enemies scatter'd round.

And if that had been too little,
  More for him he would have done,
If he had kept each tittle
  Of the law, like Christ His son.

Jesus, in his warfare, conquer'd,
  He the tempter did dethrone;
His kingdom he has enter'd,
  And he soon will reign alone.

When the Church in new apparel,
  For her spouse is really drest,
God will wean man from his idol,
  And give earth her heav'nly rest.

King David's Son on earth will reign,
  On Mount Zion's holy hill;
Then sin God will with iron chain,
  And his love in our hearts instill.

Hasten then, his throne is waiting,
  The elect are all prepar'd,
O delay not your repenting,
  Or your souls will be ensnar'd.

THE FIRST TEMPLE.

The first Eve brought much sorrow to man,
Disarrang'd th' Almighty's plan;
She did what she should not have done,—
The great web of evil spun.

She shut the windows of heaven,
She fill'd our hearts with leaven,
She put a vail over our eyes
Which our body petrifies.

When sin and sinners did abound,
God with water hid the ground;
God opened his windows in wrath,
And cover'd the earth with froth.

One man, call'd Noah, God did spare
As he did an ark prepare,
And seven others, for his sake,
He did with him in it take.

'Mid heaven and earth, this floating ark—
This one little, lonely bark
Held all, in love, that God could save
From a dreadful, watery grave.

For sin had so mankind disgrac'd,
That God them almost effac'd.
Noah, alone, his God obey'd,
So his family were sav'd.

Through jeers and taunts this ark was made;
Ponder well and be afraid!
One man, one ark, the race preserv'd,
When from truth the rest had swerv'd.

That one did faithfully fulfil
In all things his Maker's will;
The length, the breadth, the height, he made
By the rule God for him laid.

One door, one window did it grace,
And three stories found a place;
Rooms in compartments did divide—
God did all its movements guide.

A little spark of light does gleam
From this little tiny thing—
Fit emblem of the temple, where
God hears and answers prayer.

Had Noah kept the ark well clos'd,
Death had never interpos'd,
For while within it they did rest,
Death did never them molest.

But, when he to the earth return'd,
The first sacrifice he burned
Show'd symptoms of an evil heart,
Which death's shadows did impart.

The fathers, each, and all, did raise
Altars, the Lord God to praise;
Like Abel they did sacrifice
Blood, whose incense reached the skies.

But still, Death did these fathers take
Across his mysterious lake;
And ever since he has prevail'd,
And his woes on man entail'd.

When God to Moses had made known
How he should for sin atone,
He built an altar 'neath a hill,
Blood upon and 'round did spill;

Twelve pillars there did represent
The twelve tribes, who, penitent,
To God their offerings did bring,
Which from thankful hearts did spring.

For they did all, with one accord,
Promise to obey the Lord;
The people did God's presence feel,
He his glory did reveal.

A tabernacle, then, we see,
Where these tribes did bend the knee,—
A covering which God desir'd,
And his holy things requir'd.

Ten curtains did to it pertain,
Which were parted just in twain,
With five on each side, so entwin'd
That they were, it seems, design'd

To cover all the means of grace,
Center'd in this hallow'd place;
Whose door God's glory did defend
When their worship did ascend.

Whenever man to God does pray
Satan in his cunning way
Inserts some little secret sin,
That some homage he may win.

Soon Israel's sons their pride betray—
For an earthly king they pray;
To their request he did accede
After he with them did plead.

God as their king they did reject,
Saul he for them did select;
Samuel did with oil anoint,
After God did him appoint.

But Saul did fail God's word to keep,
Sin did all his senses steep,
And God another king did name,
Bidding Samuel him proclaim.

David, the second Jewish King,
Did conceive a wondrous thing;
To goodness he his heart inclin'd,
The first temple he design'd.

And for it he did well prepare,
Silver, gold, and jewels, rare;
But, it from building did refrain,
For he had so many slain.

The temple, that God's glory fill'd,
Solomon, his son, did build;
With beauteous wood and fine-hewn stone,
This glorious temple shone.

In every country, now, we find
Temples of all sorts and kind;
But none can, like the first one, show
The fire which in it did glow,

Nor does God's glory in them shine
As it did in former time;
Some reason there must surely be
Why these things we cannot see.

We now no sacrifice do need,
Christ for all the good does plead;
But oh! let all together pray
For a beam of that lost ray.

But, alas! the Devil has made
The temple his grand arcade;
He has made men believe, with pride,
There in priests they should confide.

Memorials of the human kind
In it, ev'rywhere, we find;
God's glory these must much efface,
This is not their proper place.

Apostles, prophets, martyrs, saints
With great care the artist paints,
The house of God to beautify,
But they really testify

How sadly we do magnify
Acts by which we glorify
The great and mighty King of kings,
From whom ev'ry creature springs.

Thus in each church he finds a place
Where he does himself encase;
This place he must at once resign
When we all our prayers entwine.

United, we will him defy,
And the Church will purify;
Jesus will then his people guide,
And his Church become his bride.

Malachi says, that when we pay
God his tithes, in his own way,
Heav'ns windows will open wide,
God will bless instead of chide.

LOT'S WIFE.

Remember, I pray,
That terrible day,
When Sodom, with flame,
Lit up all the plain.

Then, think of Lot's wife,
How she lost her life;
She knew, well, the way,
But wish'd for delay.

One lingering look,—
Death her overtook;
She God disobey'd—
Her soul thus betray'd.

Her frame then became
A pillar of shame;
Banished for ever—
One stroke did sever

From friend and from foe,
To regions of woe;
Take warning by this!
For moments of bliss

Do not sacrifice
Your heavenly prize—
With Zoar in sight
Had she been upright,

Her name with renown
Would be handed down;
Fly, then, to Zoar!
There is but one door.

If we put away pride,
The Spirit will guide,
And give us the grace
Sin lost to the race.

THE TABERNACLE WITH THE COURT AND CAMP.

A The Tabernacle. B The Laver. C The Altar of burnt offering.
D The Court. E The Cloud of Glory.

DEAR JEWISH FRIENDS,—

Your believe that man was first tempted by a woman under the influence of the serpent, who of course, was the Evil Spirit. We Christians believe that our Christ was the Lamb slain from the foundations of the world. The Lamb, typified in Isaac, who died that we might live, who took upon him our nature and was born of a woman, conceived of the Holy Spirit. Would that God might enable me, a mere woman as I am, and one who has been led through the wilderness of this world by the special providence of God for many years, through, I may say, as strange trials and troubles as have ever fallen to the lot of a human being, to lift from your eyes the veil which hides from you a Saviour's love. My object in writing is not to open a controversy, but to induce you to search the scriptures and see if Christ has not fulfilled those prophecies which has, since the days of your father Abram, led you to look for a perfect human sacrifice for sin, so that Moses, in whom you trust, shall not accuse you hereafter, for Christ said "Had ye believed Moses ye would have believed me.—John v. 46. As soon as your people kneel to Christ in faith the reign of truth will dawn upon the earth and Christ's spiritual reign begins. As the Messiah Christ will then return, either personally or spiritually, to be our king, and reign over you in Jerusalem, the Holy City.

My subject, then, is—

"CHRIST, THE SON OF GOD."

Text—John 8, 14. "Though I bear record of myself yet my record is true; for I know whence I came and whither I go."

A Unitarian tract before me, by W. G. Eliot, D.D., (written with the object of proving that Christ was without the divine nature of God,) takes this same text; but in how different a light do I see it. None but God could know whence He came or whither He went. None of the inspired men of the Old Testament knew it, nor does any one living know it. God, in His mercy, has sent us His Bible as a rule of life, that we might first learn to know His will, and then practise it. All efforts to keep the law perfectly in the best living creature must fall far short of what God requires. Therefore, Christ appeared himself to your fathers in the form of a man, and then condescended to be born of a pure virgin, fulfilling, in every particular, the Prophecy of Isaiah, (Isaiah vii. 14) for God's justice required a sacrifice; so the second person in the blessed Trinity came in the person of Jesus Christ to wash away our sins in His blood to purify and prepare our bodies for the indwelling of the Holy Spirit, and "by one offering he hath perfected forever them that are sanctified," (Hebrews x. 14.) Though the Devil had the great power to ruin the beautiful creature that God had made, still the power that made had the power to restore. The redemption of the world is a work of wonderful love and mercy, so complete that man can neither add anything to it nor take anything from it. God now offers us greater happiness and beauty than we lost,—giving us, however, the free will to choose whether we will have for our Father God, who loves us, or the Devil, who hates us. As He said to your fathers He now says to us—"Choose ye this day whom ye will serve."

The Devil hates us because he once had all those joys as his own which Christ has now prepared for us; he having lost them, does not choose that we shall ever enjoy them. Christianity, thank God, to those who have at times felt the power of the Holy Trinity on the soul, is so far beyond all human philosophy that none but those who have felt its power, feel that there are no words in which to express it, but Christ's own words to Nicodemus—"Ye must be born of water and of the Spirit,"—which must have been intended to teach the use of baptism instead of circumcision, in this, obeying the law, which obedience will lead you to believe the Gospel, and see in Christ the Messiah for whom you still look.

To sit at the feet of Jesus, to learn His will, as the Unitarians do, from His human nature instead of His divine, reminds me of a child going to a lesson of any sort with the hope of learning that lesson by the teacher merely reading it to him,—if it was music, playing it for him, or a language, speaking it to him, or drawing, sketching it for him. No faith to believe that the teacher is a being, composed of body, mind, and soul or spirit,—endowed with the power of imparting that knowledge and of fixing it as it were on the mind or soul for ever.

Now, this is a mystery. Can you explain it? No. Do you believe it? Yes. God is a spirit. God made man, (we are told by Moses in Genesis,) after His own image. If, then, you believe that you are made of three parts—body, mind, and soul, why cannot you believe that God made us by His power, justified us by His love, and in mercy sanctified us by His Holy Spirit, so that by the action of all the Three in One who made us, God's justice might be appeased?

The world is beginning to grow old; time is hastening us on to the end of all things. Would it not be wise, instead of trying to find out whether the world was built in six days or as many thousand years—why God has not informed us more on this subject and more on that—why this was not put in the Old Testament and that left out of the New? I repeat it, would it not be wiser to try to become more humble, loving Christians, striving to follow out the

God-like graces of the Saviour,—looking at him as he is,—the beautiful picture of what Adam was before the fall,—as also, of God's revealed will to man, which he gave to Moses on the Mount on two tables of stone? If Christ were not God, why did He come at all, and why as a child? We knew our duty from the law, and we have no more power now to keep it perfectly than before Christ came. God's justice required a perfect sacrifice for sin, to do away with your many sacrifices and to reconcile us to himself,—to purify, to wash us from our sins. His coming as a man would have been quite useless, for we know that a person may be very moral without being at all religious. Christ does not say you must keep the law to the letter or you will never see the Lord; but it is said "without holiness no man shall see the Lord." Our hearts tell us that of ourselves we are not holy, then there was need of a sacrifice and that a holy one. The angels are not perfect, or Satan would not have fallen; hence the reason why Christ came and suffered, and ere he returns to reign God's Holy Spirit will make us holy. That God's ways are mysterious none will deny; but yet a humble, trusting Christian finds no difficulty in believing what has been revealed, and looks forward in hope to the time when our spiritual sight will be restored, and all will be made plain. The plan of redemption to him is simple. It soothes all his sorrows and drives away all his cares. The feeling that his soul reposes in a Saviour's arms, and that in His holiness he shall appear before his God, is to him greater riches than all the glory and honor of the world.

Pride, the cause of the Devil's own fall, is his principal weapon, which he uses to draw souls from God. There are so many varieties of pride, or, rather, Satan tempts us by it in so many different ways, that we seldom know when it influences our actions. It is pride that tempts a Unitarian to call himself a Christian, when it would become him better to take some Jewish name, or, if he could, to join the Jewish Church. It would, I think be more consistent, for at baptism the Christian has three privileges conferred upon him:—1st. He who was naturally estranged from Christ is made a member of Him,—that is, a member of that mystical body whereof Christ is the head. (Ephesians ii. 12.) 2nd. He who was naturally a child of wrath is now made a son of God by adoption through Christ, the Son of God by nature. (Galatians iv. 5.) 3rd. Being a son of God, he who was naturally a child of perdition is now made an heir of God and joint heir with Christ to a kingdom of glory. Now, if a Unitarian does not believe this, how can he be a Christian? We do not take our family name because we are obedient children. We must be of the same nature, born into the same family. Then, how can we take the name of Christ without having been baptized, which alone distinguishes us from Jews, Turks, and Infidels? Our keeping the law does not make us Jews; nor can a Unitarian become a Christian by leading a life more like Christ than Christians do. Nothing can make a man what he is not made by the form prescribed; and I do not think that anything but being born a Jew can make one a Jew, nor can any one be a Christian unless baptized of *water* and the *Spirit*. Anything else is a delusion of the Evil One to entrap their souls. Nothing but divine power could have fulfilled, as Christ did, all the ancient prophecies which are contained in the Old Testament concerning the Messiah. It required divine power to perform the miracles which he did. Then, again, the holiness of the doctrine which he prescribed, banishing idolatry, superstition and vice out of the world, and teaching instead the knowledge and worship of the true God, the fulfilling of the law, and the practice of all manner of virtues. He showed, also, His divine power by His resurrection, for He remained on earth forty days, eating and drinking with His disciples, and appearing suddenly unto them when they neither knew "whence He came or whither He went;" His wonderful ascension into Heaven, by which He finished the fulfilment of the prophecies regarding himself which He delivered while on earth, of which His disciples, once Jews themselves, were the living witnesses.

Add to this the testimony of Josephus, who says— (Book 18, chapter 3)—"that Jesus was a wise man, if it be lawful to call him a man, for He did wonderful works: He taught men to receive the truth with pleasure; He drew over to Him many of the Jews. He was Christ, and Pilate condemned Him to the cross on the 3rd April. Those that loved Him did not forsake Him,* for He appeared to them alive again the third day, April 5th, as the divine prophets had foretold these and ten thousand other wonderful things concerning Him."

You, yourselves, are a text to us. It is not an inspired man that you expect. It is God himself; and because Christ did not come with pomp and great glory, you cannot believe Him to be the Messiah. He often appeared to your fathers. They did not doubt that it was He, and their faith was much stronger than ours, for they believed in what had not then happened. Now your people find it hard to believe what has come to pass.

The fearful destruction of your temple, city, and

---

* He really should have said, "those he loved he did not forsake, for he appeared to them alive again, the third day after his crucifixtion, and now having finished his work of Redemption, he must and will return to finish his work of Glorification which he has begun, and when finished, man will be a perfectly Holy being, living like Christ did while on earth."

commonwealth by the Romans, which Christ foretold you forty years before it took place (Luke xxi. 20); your being scattered about upon the earth and remaining as you are to this day, as prophecied by Hosea in his 3rd chapter, without a king, without a high priest, and without a temple, without a sacrifice,—for you have had none since Christ came,—are living monuments and witnesses to the truth of these prophecies. Then see, for three hundred years after Christ's ascension, the Holy Spirit gave the Apostles power to preach the Gospel to all nations in their own language, and to work miracles. These days are passed, but Christ still assists the humble Christian in his efforts to be good; and no matter how often he fails, if he only turns to Him in true penitence and prayer, "He is able to save them to the uttermost also that come unto God by Him, seeing He ever liveth to make intercession for them." (Hebrews vii. 25). But if we will not hear Moses and the prophets, neither will we be persuaded though one rose from the dead. (Luke xvi.)

Some Unitarians ask the question, Are we disciples of Christ or only first among equals? The Gospel teaches us to believe *in* Jesus, (the word Jesus means a Saviour.) Why? Because He is the Saviour of mankind, (Acts iv, 12,) and He is called Anointed because called to three offices, that of Prophet, Priest, and King. As a Prophet, Christ instructs His Church outwardly by His Word, (Luke 4, 18,) and inwardly by His Spirit (John xiv. 26. As a Priest, He reconciles by His death on the cross, (1 Timothy 25,) as also by His continual intercession to God for us; and as a King, He governs and protects His people and Church (Ephesians ii. 22,) but has not yet claimed his victory over death. To Christ, also, may be applied the attributes which belong to God,—1st. The attribute of unchangableness, for in John 8, 58, he says, " Before Abraham was, I am." 2nd. The attribute of Omnipresence, for He told His disciples that He would be with them to the end of the world. His sovereignty I have already proved.

If Christ had not been divine, He could not have told the woman of Samaria what she had done. Remember how the disciples felt their hearts burning within them when He talked to them after His resurrection. Faith would be of no value if the mystery were not very great. We cannot comprehend God now, but we can easily believe that He could take our nature on Him if He chose. All nations worship some sort of a god. To worship the true God, then, does not require much faith. The beauty of faith can only be shown in the belief of God's wonderful love and mercy in loving us so much who love him so little, and in suffering for us so much agony. What man could have borne the agony of all the sins of the world, when the remorse of one sin will sometimes drive a person to despair? Then He contended, as it were, with the Evil One and overcame. What man can do this without having his soul stained with sin? The Evil One seems, as it were, to throw a veil for a time over our eyes; in fact, to make us believe that we are doing right when we are doing wrong—that we are saints when we are.greater sinners than those who have, perhaps, less pretensions; and it is only by constant prayer and the help of God's Holy Spirit that one is able to struggle and tear oneself from his grasp. All the inspired men in the Old Testament have fallen under the power of Satan at one time or another. Moses lost his temper several times; he even slew an Egyptian. Abraham's faith failed him before Abimeleck. Isaac failed the same way. Jacob told a lie and deceived his poor old father. David and Solomon both sinned exceedingly before the Lord. So that the fact of Christ being inspired would not have been sufficient to have enabled Him to contend against the

Evil One as He did, Christ showed dependence on God in His human nature, which would not have been complete without it. Christ came to set before us a perfect example of Adam before the Fall, as also a loving picture of God's will to man once given on stone. He kept the law perfectly. Close your eyes and look at Christ in this way—the perfection of all that is lovely and beautiful can give but a very faint idea of His beauty. If the Christian combines the faith of the Jew and the Unitarian, we prove Christ to be divine. The Jews, by their strong belief that the Messiah must be God himself, with the veil still over their eyes, fulfilling Christ's own prophecy concerning them, and of which He warned them (Matthew xiii. 13); then the Unitarian, by proving that Christ fulfilled prophecies and obeyed the law to the letter, proves Him to be the Messiah for whom the Jews still look; for, in offering Himself upon the cross in the person of His Son, He proves himself to be the Saviour of the world. These two faiths, then, prove the doctrine of the Trinity. Indeed, it seems plain that if Christ was not God no man will be saved; for, without the divine nature was complete in Christ, no man will appear before God.

As soon as the Jew learns to know that the Messiah has come, I believe he will put to shame the Christians of the present day, whose faith is certainly not that of Abraham, nor their deeds those which St. Paul taught. How plainly both Jew and Gentile, in their unbelief, follow up Adam's great sin of pride; both are too proud to believe that God took upon Him the nature of man, whom he made after His own image, as if all things are not possible with God. If we could once feel His love—a love so great that, when enduring the most intense agony, He cried out, "Father, forgive them, for they know not what they do,"—so great that He ever liveth to make intercession for us, (Hebrews vii. 25) and so immense that through Him, St. John says, "we have become the sons of God," and yet we are not changed in appearance but in his first epistle, he tells us " that we shall see Him as He is when we are made like Him."

" I am the way, the truth and the life." It seems to me that Christ has made the way clear. The Holy Spirit plants the truth in our hearts, and God is the life. Christ was circumcised to fulfil the law, and He was baptized to set us an example of the sacrament that He wished to introduce, which was to take the place of circumcision in the Christian Church. " Go ye and baptize all nations in the name of the Father, the Son, and the Holy Ghost." The Father sends the Son, and He imparts the Holy Spirit. All three persons here hold a personal office, and are all three made equal. The baptism is to comprise all three, and then follows the promise—" Lo, I am with you always, even unto the end of the world." Yes, He is with us to guide us and keep us from the Evil Spirit, whose constant employment is to hinder us from doing good and to induce us to do evil (Galatians v. 17; Romans vii. 23). Some Gentiles say there is no Devil or Evil Spirit; then how do they account for their evil thoughts and actions? If there is one, then ask yourself what would be most likely his first object. To keep us from knowing God. He will try as he did with Adam to persuade us that some one of his attributes are superior to the other—either His mercy will save us without the appointed means, or His love will show itself in a different way from what He has told us himself, or His justice did not require that He should come himself, as He has done. These are the wicked suggestions which he deludes us with. Are they not the same as the one with which he tempted Adam? " Ye shall not surely die;" but has that prevented us from dying? Although Adam, like his children, was foolish enough to believe him, still, has it altered the sentence? Does not every day, hour, minute, and second testify to the truth of God and the success of the Devil's works?

Take an example of any good work,—we will say the building of a church. Look at the way Solomon's temple was built. Look at the offerings that King Solomon brought to God before he commenced to built it. Then see how the people answered to Solomon's call in 1st Kings 5-9. Hiram says:—"I have considered the things which thou sentest to me for, and I will do all thy desire; my servants shall bring down the timber from Lebanon to the sea." And all he asks in return is food for his men. See the gold that the Queen of Sheba brought. Now, look at the way we build churches to the Lord. First, the Devil tries to make the congregation who wish to build it quarrel among themselves, by this means to prevent it being built at all. Then, when the time has come that God chooses the church shall be built, he does all he can by his devices so to influence them and their work as to make it a temple for God in *name* only, for one man will give the land for the purpose of improving his property; the money will be given by the people to the praise of their own names; the minister will get it built to show what great power he has, and how he rules his people; and then there will be constant contention among themselves. Is this, I ask, working for God's glory or the praise of His holy name?

But the day is at hand. The Jews in Jerusalem will build again the temple of the Lord,—a temple, I believe, which has had none so beautiful since the one that King Solomon built,—and where both prayer and praise will rise to the Triune God from the hearts and souls of the worshippers. God grant that I may live to see it, for this temple will begin to be built as soon as the Jews can see that the Messiah has come indeed, and that Jesus Christ was the Son of God, who came to earth in His human nature and offered himself on the cross for our salvation.

In Deuteronomy xxi. 23, every one that is hanged on a tree is cursed. In Galatians iii. 13, it says, "Christ hath redeemed us from the curse of the law." The angel of the Lord, who spoke twice to Abraham out of Heaven, was no other than Christ, who told the Jews himself, in John viii. 56, that "your Father Abraham rejoiced to see my day, and he saw it and was glad." Job, in xxxi. 31, said, "Oh, that we had of His flesh." We cannot be satisfied; we have it and will not take it. The Jews in Christ's day asked (John vi. 52), How can this man give us His flesh to eat? and Christ said, "my flesh is meat indeed, and my blood is drink indeed." Although the death of many saints and righteous persons have testified to the truth of these words, how many cannot be satisfied because they will not believe. Christians are apt to think that because the Jewish nation actually put our Lord to death that they are very wicked; but St. Paul says, in Hebrews, "for it is impossible for those who were once enlightened and have tasted of the Heavenly gift, and were made partakers of the Holy Ghost, and have tasted the good Word of God and the powers of the world to come,—if they shall fall away to renew them again unto repentance seeing they crucify to themselves the Son of God afresh, and put him to an open shame."

Jews and Gentiles both saw Him go into Heaven, where He now sits at the right hand of God, there to intercede and to accept from us our smallest and most imperfect services done for His sake. All will again see Him when He comes to judge the quick and the dead; but before that time the following prophecies together with numberless others must be fulfilled. "For though Thy people Israel be as the sands of the sea, yet a remnant of them shall return." Isaiah x. 22.

"Be still and know that I am God: I will be exalted among the Heathen, I will be exalted in the earth."—Psalm 46, 10.

"In his days shall the righteous flourish: and abundance of peace so long as the moon endureth."— 72. Ps. vii.

"It shall come to pass in the last days, that the mountain of the Lord's house shall be established in the top of the mountains and shall be exalted above the hills; and all nations shall flow unto it."—Isaiah ii. 2.

"He will swallow up death in victory; and the Lord God will wipe away tears from all faces: and the rebuke of his people shall he take away from off all the earth: for the Lord hath spoken it."—Isaiah xxv. 8.

If it is our Father's will that Esau's sons should gather his wheat into his garner and collect the crumbs that are lying under his table, thus regaining our lost birthright and breaking Jacob's yoke from off their necks, let me beseech you to apply yourselves at once to this, great, wondrous work. Search well this book, and if it proves to you that Christ was divine, he must be the Messiah for whom you still look, and when your people acknowledge him as such he will put on his glorious apparel and will come from Edom with dyed garments from Bozrah, and Isaiah's beautiful description of the milennium time to be found in lxv. chap. 17 and following verses will be seen and enjoyed by those who have died, and those who then live in the faith of God's own beloved Son of whom St. Paul says in Colossians i. 15: "He is the image of the invisible God, the first born of every creature, for by Him were all things created. He then goes on to show that He reconciled us to God by His death on the cross, and also shows that by His Holy Spirit even those who are *aliens* and enemies will be brought to trust and believe in him.

Although the subject to me seems exhaustless, still, I think I have written enough to show that Christ had, while on earth, the dignity, authority, and power belonging to God; and, therefore, that His divine nature was complete. That it is a great mystery none can deny; but that we must believe in it, if we ever wish to see God and dwell with Him, is a fact which Scripture clearly proves; and if God, as God, requires His justice to be satisfied; if, as Christ, He has shown His love and requires ours in return; if, as the Holy Spirit, He is willing to come in mercy, and only asks us to pray for His help, why cannot we humble ourselves to see things as He chooses,— be like little children, "humble, teachable, and mild," willing to learn in the way God chooses for us, even though it is not exactly the way that will satisfy our pride of intellect, or pride of any or every sort. We know that "we now see through a glass darkly, but then face to face." Now we know in part, but then shall we know also as we are known. There is evidently something kept back; we are not now intended to know everything. Now we are to trust and believe, so as to prepare us gradually to see and know God as He is—the Alpha and Omega—the beginning and the end—the first and the last.

"Blessed are they that do His commandments, that they may have right to the Tree of Life, and may enter in through the gates into the City,—that City where there is no night, for the Lord God giveth them light, and they shall reign for ever and ever."

  Come, Jews, behold the end draws near,
   The world on thee doth wait,
  As soon as you can see and hear,
   Christ and his church will mate.

He left his Father's throne above,
　And learnt our childish ways,
He showed us how to live and love
　Virtue's glorious ways.

These ways which draw us near to God,
　Unite us link by link,
Will cause our feet to be so shod
　Nothing can make us sink.

The holy fire that Moses saw,
　That on your altar shone,
Will purify all nature's laws;
　And place Christ on his throne.

Instead of trying to unite
　Death's citadel to storm—,
Each takes a flint and strikes a light,
　Which gives Death no alarm.

When Christians, with united hearts,
　God's temple do embrace,
With torches full of fiery darts!
　Death they from earth will chase.

Our sins to the cross are nailed;
　Jesus has pierc'd death's sting,
Christians hitherto have fail'd
　To fasten on death's wings.

37TH EZEKIEL.

I see with the prophet's eyes
　The dry bones which he did see;
All around earth's valley lies
　A dead Christianity.

But the breath of God will soon
　Each bone to his bone unite,—
Skin, sinews, and flesh, assume
　Some great new power and might.

"Come from the four winds, O Breath'
  And awake these sleeping bones,
Snatch them from the arms of death,
  And make them glittering stones.

Whose united, steady light,
  Will unmask the pomps of earth,
And together burning bright,
  Prove them to be nothing worth.

For such radiance will shine
  From the tabernacle then,
That the riches of God's mine
  Will attract all sorts of men.

Israel then will seek the fold,
  Christ the Shepherd they will own;
Again, as in the days of old,
  God will as their King be known.

THE LOST TRIBES.

And have we really found the lost
  Ten Tribes so often sought,
Are Briton's sons the mighty host,
  The ones that Christ has taught.

If this is true the time draws nigh
  For Esau's sons to wake,
To take the bands from off their eyes,
  And Jacob's yoke to break.

Two names our Father Jacob bore,
  Two nations thus have sprung,
The Britons and the Turks of yore
  Must all from him have come.

Then Jews at once the cross upraise,
  The crescent then will wane,
When you Messiah learn to praise,
  And bow at Jesus' name.

You will your glory all attain,
   The tribes will reunite,
God's ten commands will then regain
   Their pure and long lost light.

When Esau's sons their birthright win
   The Serpent's race is run,
Hearts then all purified from sin,
   Will his devices shun.

PALESTINE.

See, look through space to Palestine,
While I now to you define
What now is seen in this fair land,
Desolate on ev'ry hand.

Four belts this country now divide,
Mediterranean on its side;
Fine foliage all around is seen,
Trees of many shades of green.

Moving along on Arab steed,
Mules behind with all your need;
The tracts the animals have made
Guide one through its lonely shade.

Our winter frosts, with ice and snow,
This fine country doth not know,
Yet it is very lonely, sad,
Natives wild and barely clad—

Live on the hills, and clefts of rock,
All they own, a little flock,
  Though here once God's own people dwelt,
  In the greatest temple knelt.

Where Tyre's towers once soar'd on high
Fishers' nets are spread to dry;
Woes, by Prophets long foretold,
The traveller can there behold.

Atheists you must cease to sneer,
And begin our God to fear,
For on this spot of hallow'd ground
Truth of God's own word is found.

Come, open out your temple-door,
   The gospel to accept;
The Spirit will his blessings pour
   When Christ you do elect.

As King of kings, he stands and knocks,
   O, pray him enter in;
He is the great, the mighty rock,
   Who can us save from sin.

A JEWISH MOTHER'S LAMENT.

A Jewish mother, lone and sad,
   Sits mourning for her only son;
A dire disease struck down the lad!
   Just as he had great honors won.

In childhood he her rule obey'd,
   In youth he all her will fulfill'd;
His mind with learning well array'd,
   And ev'ry virtue there instill'd.

The Jews all lov'd this comely youth,
   And many thought that he might be
A leader, chosen for his truth,
   To guide their people through the sea—

Back to Jerusalem, the land
  Where once they dwelt in glory great,
With prophets, priests, on ev'ry hand,
  And kings, who sat in regal state.

No, Jewish maidens! Jewish sons,
  The glory that your people craves
Can never dawn till Christ has won
  From you belief he died to save.

As soon as this, with faith, you see,
  Your ancient glory will return,
The Holy Land then soon will be
  The place to which you will sojourn.

All then will see Christ's holy reign,—
  He comes with sceptre to restore,
He comes to free the world from pain,
  And ev'ry blessing on us pour.

Spiritual sight that Adam lost,
  Will gently by us be regain'd;
O, let not any earthly cost
  Be valu'd till this end's attain'd.

No mother then will have to sigh,
  No husband part with his dear wife,
No father see his lov'd one die,
  All will be love, and rest and life.

This time of bliss, this glorious time
  Must be by you now brought to pass,
If you have come from Esau's line
  Your slavish days will soon be past.

Awake then, now attend my call,
  Ev'ry tie from me I fling,—
Come rouse thee, Jewish people all,
  And with me you will gaily sing.

That glorious temple you will build,
  One great altar you will raise;
All Satan's schemes to you will yield,
  And all will echo Jesus' praise.

For he was God, the mighty God
• As Prophet, Priest, he has been here;
But when he comes as King, our God,
  Man will him love and never fear.

If I God's holy people lead
  To kneel before the cross in truth,
Your Numa will with all his seed,
  Enjoy again eternal youth.

GOD'S PROVIDENCE.

What wondrous care our Father takes
  Of all his faithful flock;
He guides us when we sleep or wake,
  And winds us likes a clock.

Through trials small and trials great,
  On ev'ry side beset,
He teaches us to work and wait
  Till he his throne has set.

The seasons four in order come,
  And with them cold and heat;
Each day behold the beauteous sun,
  With rays of light we meet.

The moon with softer light to soothe,
  The stars around to cheer,
The planets as they daily move—
  All for mankind appear.

The trees alone, in summer time,
    Are clad in robes of green,
In winter they their leaves do hide,
    And gray and bare are seen.

And on the trees grow lovely fruit,
    Quite perfect in their form,
Each one with scent or taste to suit,
    Our garden to adorn.

Some good and useful sap do yield
    To comfort and sustain;
Their branches from the sun to shield,
    And shelter from the rain.

Good people, like fine trees in bloom,
    Enrich the very ground,
While dead and burnt ones cast a gloom
    And sadness all around.

We cannot nature's works assist,
    Nor can we understand,
Before our eyes there is a mist
    Which covers sea and land.

This veil, which sin has caused to grow,
    Which hides God from our eyes,
Is growing thicker, from the flow
    Of self-deceit and lies.

THE CHRISTIAN'S HOPE.

Great Spirit of this mighty world,
Who Adam thy sweet voice has heard,
Send down to earth, thy regal chair;
And reign o'er earth, sea, sky and air.

Let Jew and Gentile, Turk and slave
Learn how thou dost redeem and save;
And that thou soon will glorify
The humblest saint, though low he lie.

Yes? raise him from his dusky bed,
To join the choir by angels led,
To live a pure and holy life,
And make an end of all our strife.

Come holy spirit, come, oh! come,
Teach us all evil now to shun,
The power of gold at once destroy,
And give us joys without alloy.

Speak but the word, death's reign is o'er
Fresh blessings on thy children pour,
Sickness, pain and sorrow, all
Will flee before the angel's call.

The Tree of Life to us restore,
That we may live for evermore;
Feed us with its heavenly fruit;
And blossoms sweet will from us shoot.

THE LOVE OF GOD.

The love of God, majestic theme,
In the elements is seen,
They are the germs from which do spring,
Every moving, living thing.

Man above all was made to show,
His great glory here below,
When sin, his beauty did deface,
Love restored to him his grace.

And though man lives to disobey
His Creator, day by day,
Yet untold blessings him surround.
Treasures for him fill the ground.

For man, God keeps his garners full,
Yearly grains and fruits to cull,
But fresh supplies *their* places fill
When man does the ground well till.

In sleep his angels guard his bed
Righteous souls by him are fed,
Light cheers his spirit day by day,
On his sad and lonely way.

He sent his Son, his love to seal,
Satan's deadly wound to heal;
Streams of blood for man he shed;
His body laid among the dead.

He lives again to intercede,
And with God for man to plead,
That he would to the earth restore,
Life and joy for evermore.

GOD'S SPIRITUAL PRESENCE IN THE BREAD AND WINE.

Daily our bodies take their food,
And try to get it pure and good,
Few, very few, refuse their gold,
To buy the best that can be sold.

The earth in summer season yields
Grain, grass and fruits, in all her fields,
When God withholds his bount'ous hand,
Famine spreads all around the land.

Our souls from God must all be fed,
Or they will be by Satan led;
In faith, his presence we must see,
Or we can never happy be.

No incense now that we can buy
Will draw God from his throne on high,
Pure and united faith and love
Will make our earth like heav'n above.

God, on the Jewish mercy seat,
In the Schekinah priest did meet
The spirit there made known to man,
In fire, the great Creator's plan.

Man fail'd to work out God's design,
And lost this wondrous, mystic sign,
To save us from the Father's wrath,
Christ shed his blood upon the cross.

While on this earth, with man Christ walk'd,
And to his priests, he daily talk'd;
His holy presence left behind,
To cheer the faint and cure the blind.

The body now, the spirit wears,
Is bread and wine the altar bears,
'Tis true, God's essence fills all space,
But there he feeds us with his grace.

When once man really can believe,
He does in Sacraments receive
The food his spirit does require,
Again will glow the Holy Fire.

We show our love when we obey,
Our faith, that Christ prepar'd the way,
Our hope, that he will soon descend;
And saints and angels him attend.

He comes not now to bleed and die,
But all below to glorify;
He comes to sit as king in state,
And make the lowly Christian great.

Man yet will live for ever,
  His blood will always flow;
Nothing us from Christ will sever
  When earth is Heav'n below.

JOHN THE BAPTIST.

A righteous priest we now behold,
  A virtuous wife had he,
Zacharias his name we're told,—
  One of Aaron's daughters she.

All the commands of God they kept,
  His ordinances fulfill'd;
They lov'd his righteous precepts,—
  Truth in them was well instill'd.

Still a miracle they did need
  To open their eye of faith,
And that God did to them concede
  The narrative further saith.

This priest did at the altar burn
  Incense in the holy place,
When suddenly he does discern,
  On his right an angel's face.

Now full of dread he trembling stood,
  For the angel to him spake,
And bade him trust, for soon he shoul
  Of an earthly joy partake.

The dearest wishes of his heart
  Had reached the throne above;
The father soon would do his part
  And shower on him his love.

His lonely hearth God soon would cheer,
  For his wife would have a son
Who should be great in faith, but fear
  Now struck Zacharias dumb—

And speechless, we are told, remain'd
  Till all things had been perform'd,
Then were the things to him explain'd
  That he so before had scorn'd.

When he in God's own temple bent
  His child to circumcise,
The Holy Ghost, in quick descent,
  Miraculous grace applies.

His name is John, his father wrote,
  As the angel had desir'd;
In verse what follows, I do quote,
  As the Spirit has inspir'd:

His tongue was loos'd in praises loud,
  Good news from Heav'n to men,
Messiah comes to pierce sin's cloud,
  And the stream of sin to stem.

This John was sent men to prepare
  For the day spring from on high;
He did with moral courage dare
  Sin's temptations to defy.

In raiment, made of camel's hair,
  He all pride of life disclaim'd;
The leathern girdle he did wear
  All his other passions chain'd;

Locusts and honey were his meat—
   Such the poorest could obtain,
To him as good as finest wheat,
   While he did the Christ proclaim.

May we, like John, prepare the way,
   Subduing ourselves with toil,
Presenting quite a bright array
   Of lamps well fill'd with oil.

All burning with a strong desire
   To see the dear Bridegroom's face,
Who soon will come with holy fire,
   And give to each saint a place.

THE CHURCH OF THE FUTURE.

Christian women of all creeds
Combine to draw out all the weeds
That Satan has so slyly sown,
And in the garb of goodness grown.

Each one believes his church is right,
And does not wish for other light,
But all our lights together thrown
Would make earth blaze from zone to zone.

The light of day shines all around,
The heavens with stars of light abound;
Direct from God all light is sent,
To ev'ry one this light is lent.

A written word to man God gave,
Our souls to rescue from the grave;
Christ's perfect body bore the cross,
That we might gain what Adam lost.

The Spirit yet still strives with man,
With love bids all accept God's plan;
And use all God's own precious ore,
Unmixed with any priestly lore.

Then in a circle let us join,
And cast out all the worthless coin;
Christ will to earth again return,
When we all evil learn to spurn.

When all our passions we restrain,
New life will run through ev'ry vein;
The glory of the Lord will shine,
Through this church to ev'ry clime.

THE ORIGIN OF PUBLIC WORSHIP.

The first oblation, we are told,
   The Lord did from man receive
Caus'd Satan's nature to enfold;
   Cain, like Eve, he did deceive

To sacrifice what he thought right,
   Not the thing that God requir'd,
Then the Lord withdrew from sight;
   With rage, Satan, Cain inspir'd

His brother Abel, to destroy;
   Then the spectre death appears,
Ruining all man's earthly joys,
   And filling his eyes with tears.

Enoch did walk with God, we hear,
   So his body ne'er decay'd;
As he, his Maker did revere,
   He in glory was array'd.

Noah, when from the ark, releas'd,
   Beast and bird did sacrifice,—
This is the next atoning feast,
   And its incense pierc'd the skies.

Here the name altar first appears,
   In the sacred Holy Book,
A word which Satan never hears
   Without angry thought and look.

Both Abraham and Jacob too
   Did to God stone altars raise,
Through life they goodness did pursue,
   And the great Creator praise.

Then, after these, the Lord desir'd
   Moses one of earth to make—
All three offerings, God requir'd;
   On this altar bid him stake.

A type of Christ, whose body pure,
   Should for all the world atone;
He is the altar, firm and sure,
   That will soon, King Death dethrone.

God's sanctuary altars were
   To a tabernacle chang'd,
Which in Aaron, the high priest's care,
   Moses saw, was well arrang'd.

On it God's glory did descend,
   In a cloudy pillar round.
They worshipp'd, and did apprehend
   God in prayer would there be found.

The altar was within it plac'd,
   This the Lord did satisfy;
The five things then the altar grac'd
   Will us yet electrify.

A type to us, each one must be,
   Of our present means of grace;
Christ changed them, that he might set free
   Streams of love to Adam's race.

The ark, like any new-born babe,
   Was made to contain God's word,
With that within it firmly stayed
   Gold did it surmount and gird,

So that it seems to represent
   The regenerating power
Of water, when, with good intent,
   Baptism, the babe does shower.

Then the table of shew-bread stands
   For our spiritual food,
Which, at the altar, Christ commands,
   To be eaten for our good.

The wine we take comes from the vine,
   Whose essence in streams does flow,
With tendrils round each soul to twine,
   This Shekinah's sight does show.

The incense, with its perfume sweet,
   Like the fragrance of a home
Where love and duty joyful meet,
   And discords are never known;

Whose inmates have been join'd in one
   By a holy, sacred rite;
A blessing from above have won,
   From their holiness of life.

A stately candlestick I see,
   Whose tapers are lost to sight,
An emblem of the church to me,
   With its dim, flickering light.

But God's spirit will yet renew,
   Fresh oil he will soon employ,
To bring his precious gifts to view,
   And the veil of sin destroy.

To draw a curse upon the good,
   Balaam did seven altars raise;
But God there told him, that he should
   Bless all those who sang his praise.

Baal, we know, had altars too,
   Gideon did cast down one,
This the angel desir'd him do,
   With ten men the work was done.

An emblem of God's ten pure laws,
   Which will evil ways restrain,
And close forever death's wide jaws,
   When our lives their truth sustain.

Then holy fire again will shine,
   And upon our altars burn;
God's beloved beauteous vine,
   We will one and all discern.

Two things without the camp we find,
   Which the Christian does not need,
For Christ has both these things combined—
   He has died, and now does plead.

One altar now will satisfy,
   No laver do we require;
Our sacraments can purify,
   And fill us with inward fire.

These were the outward forms, whereby
   God signified to mankind
That his own Son should live and die,
   Satan's web of sin to bind.

But man himself must snap the chain,
    He must bruise the serpent's heel;
Till then, Christ always will refrain
    From setting on sin his seal.

The priesthood which from Aaron came,
    And which God did sanctify,
A temple afterwards did frame—
    The Great God did glorify.

The tabernacle mov'd around
    This temple solid and staid,
With strong foundations underground,
    Immoveable was made.

King Solomon this temple rear'd,
    King David did it design,
When God in glory there appear'd
    Holy fire did in it shine.

Mount Moriah, King David chose
    This great temple's site to be,
For there his incense once arose,
    Which caus'd pestilence to flee.

And where the brazen serpent stood
    Until Hezekiah's reign,—
Which was a monument of good,
    To destroy the serpent's pain.

Then Abraham's great offering
    On this very spot was made,
His only son he here did bring,
    But his sacrifice God stay'd.

This temple, rich with gems and gold,
    Built of finest wood and stone,
By hearts who lavish'd wealth untold,
    Yet for sin could not atone.

The worship could not have been pure,
  Some lingering idol shar'd;
To make our earthly temple sure,
  God to us his own Son spar'd,

That we might, like him, learn to live,
  To love, worship and obey;
Our hearts into his keeping give,
  And trust him day by day.

Man's first great temple was destroy'd
  By the pillage fire and swords,
Which Babylonian's king employ'd
  To augment his strength and hoards.

The riches, and the labour, all
  That King Solomon had spent,
Was doom'd, and, like a fallen star,
  None could tell the way it went.

Years passed this desolated place,
  Nehemiah did revive;
The city he by night did pace,
  And by day with men did strive,

Till his great faith and works, at length,
  This temple did rebuild;
God blessed him, and gave him strength,
  And with courage him instill'd.

The second temple ne'er obtain'd
  The glory the first beheld;
A veil had then God's light restrain'd,
  And his holy fire withheld.

The tables on which Moses wrote
  The laws God to him made known,
God to another never spoke,
  Nor again bid write on stone.

L

Urim and Thummim, from whence came
  Answers from the King Divine,
Which to the High Priest did proclaim
  God's will by some unknown sign.

These with the gift of prophecy,
  Which soon after pass'd away,
Do very clearly specify
  A want of heavenly ray,

Which the first temple did pervade,
  And its beauty much enhance;
But mankind did so retrogade
  These did not their souls entrance.

Prayer-houses,* Proseuchai call'd,
  Spread around about this time;
In fields and mountains there install'd,
  To Heaven their thoughts did climb.

In towns and cities synagogues
  Were in use throughout the land,
And many were the demagogues
  Which in them did reprimand.

When God in mercy sent his Son
  Man to try and teach his will;
But even this beloved one
  Man has not restrain'd from ill.

---

* Synagogues were sometimes called prayer-houses, yet there were prayer-houses called Proseuchai, which differed from synagogues in three respects:—1st, They were used occassionally for private devotions,; 2nd, they had walls, but were open to the sky; and, 3rd, they were built in fields and mountains, while synagogues were only built in towns and cities. It was perhaps in one of these prayer-houses our Saviour spent his night in prayer.

Though by his life he testified
   His power and might divine,—
By death and resurrection tried
   Satan's throne to undermine,

But still within men's hearts sin reigns,—
   Earthly glories make men toil,—
Satan with gold his sway maintains,
   And the Spirit's reign does foil.

So though the Church that Christ did plant
   Fresh leaves has before us spread,
As formerly we pray and chant,
   And by Satan's wiles are led;

For Christ's sacraments have not bloom'd,
   Their flowers are not yet seen,—
For Satan and his reign are doom'd
   When Christ's blossoms here do gleam.

The shepherds did God's glory see
   When the Virgin and her Babe,
With faith and great humility,
   In a common manger laid;

For God's first prophecy to man
   Then about to be reveal'd,
His wondrous, great redemption's plan,
   Drew forth his wondrous shield.

Christ's triumph over evil deeds
   Surely bruised the serpent's head,
And his example mankind leads
   All in virtue's paths to tread.

Money-changers he did eject
   From the temple, with a scourge,
And twelve apostles did select
   These abuses all to purge.

The keys of goodness in their hands,
   Through St. Peter, he did place,
Himself the rock on which still stands
   The Church that will free man's race.

When reunited, it does show
   The power of destroying sin—
Then the latter house will glow
   With sin's antidote within.

Fulfilling Haggai's prophecy,
   Written many years ago,—
That God his house would glorify,
   And Satan's power overthrow.

Many prophecies, we well know,
   Our Saviour has explain'd,
The others he will to us show
   When his precepts are maintain'd.

Write at once upon all hearts
   God's commands that Moses wrote,
Christ said they made the two great charts
   By which all must steer and float.

He their great beauty did portray,
   All his life by them did guide,
He suffered for them day by day,
   And to teach us them he died.

That all men might enjoy again
   The happiness Adam lost,
Without the sorrow, woe and pain,
   His sins all the race have cost.

Then let us fill our hearts with love,
   For our God to reign supreme,
His Holy Spirit, like a dove,
   Will then on each head be seen.

His temple—one great blaze of light,—
  Like a beacon will appear;
Then Zion's hill will be a sight
  That the human race will cheer.

A valley only did divide
  Moriah from David's hill,
Majestically side by side,
  They with awe our thoughts do fill.

Solomon did these hill unite,
  His bridge did this valley span;
May Christ's great love the Jews incite
  To embrace redemption's plan.

For when the Jew and Christian join,
  The mountains will together meet,
And Satan with his worthless coin
  Be trodden underneath their feet.

Baal's altars do still retain
  Upon this our earth a place,
Then the angel will exclaim,
  Of Baal leave not a trace!

Pray, then, that all will soon grow wise,
  Put from them every sin,
And use their energies and eyes,
  Crowns of righteousness to win.

A PRAYER.

When to thy temple Lord we haste,
Make our thoughts both wise and chaste;
O teach us when we bend our knees,
Thee alone to try and please.

Let our spirits soar far above,
Draw them with the cords of love;
Take Satan's poison from our veins,
With thy blood wash out the stains.

We lay our souls within thy arms,
Earthly grandeur's lost its charms,
The world seems hollow and untrue,
Quickly come and make things new.

How blind and deaf man has become
To the work that thou hast done;
Creation groan'd thou didst redeem,
From sin thou did'st try to wean.

Each one his idol tightly grasps,
Gladly does the devil's tasks,
With iron chains he binds their feet,
As each victim he does cheat.

The web of sin which he does weave
Causes ev'ry pulse to heave,
The sweets that he man gives to taste,
Guides him to the grave with haste.

But in thy house there is a peace,
There earth's trials all do cease;
Our hearts seem there to fill with love,
Cheer'd with voices from above.

THIS SCROLL
IS ADDRESSED BY THE AUTHORESS
TO HIS HOLINESS
POPE PIUS THE NINTH.

MAY IT PLEASE YOUR HOLINESS.

The great trials that you have endured since you called together your Bishops to consult with you on holy things, and the division which your calling yourself infallible has caused in your branch of the Christian church, may, perhaps, have prepared your mind to re-consider the subject, I therefore again take the liberty of bringing it before you with other subjects of grave importance. For the Heathen will never embrace the doctrines of Christianity while we are a house divided against itself, but when together, we put away Pride and search for Truth, we will become a light to lighten the Gentiles, and the glory of the people of Israel. I beseech you, take God's Holy Word and see what it says about man's past, present and future state. Let us carry back our minds to that time when God, having prepared this beautiful world, one lovely garden containing all that the eye delights to behold, created and placed in it a perfect man, pure and holy, a little lower than the angels, who received one command from God Himself, not to eat the fruit of one tree in the garden. To make him completely happy, Eve was given to be his comforter and companion. The Bible does not say that God talked with Eve, but it does say that she knew the command; the serpent must have known it also. Whether the privilege of seeing, walking and talking with God was enjoyed by Adam alone, we cannot say: or, whether man was made by God to fill the place of those angels "which kept not their first estate," but left their own habitation, we can only conjecture.

Peter and Jude inform us that angels were cast out of heaven, and Matthew xxv. 41 says that hell was prepared for them; so that it was with very bitter feelings that they saw man in such a glorious world. The serpent is said to have been subtle, which means easily penetrated, so the Devil hid himself in the serpent, and tempted Eve to disobey God, under the plea of acquiring knowledge. Then she persuaded Adam. The Devil, thus using three instruments, the serpent, Eve and Adam, who he filled with unbelief, pride and disobedience, the very arts he uses with all mankind; it brought three curses on the serpent, mankind and the earth, which was God's work of the 3rd, 5th and 6th days, which three figures, by placing man before beast, make 365, the exact number of days in the year, so that they, perhaps, are under the curse. The sun, moon, stars, sky and heaven, still retain their original beauty, though clouds sometimes hide them from our gaze. But God loved man so much that while he passed the sentence of death on his body he promised a Saviour for his soul, who would be an antidote, as it were, which would prevent the poison from affecting his everlasting state, provided man tried to please God, washed away his sins in the blood of Christ, and partook of the food which Christ commanded for the strengthening and refreshing of his soul; but even this will not make him infallible. For David prays, in the 19th Psalm, to be made to understand his errors, to be cleansed from his secret sins, and to be kept back from presumptuous sins. The clouds, in different ways, often hide from our eyes the glory and beauty of the sun; flying clouds may represent our errors, a haze may signify our secret sins, and the heavy storm our presumptuous sins; but to be left without the sun, as they were at the time of the flood, is but a faint idea of perpetual banishment from the presence from God. This will be everlasting misery. There are many kinds of serpents, and they are divided into two classes, those who crush their victims to death and those who poison them. Now, supposing that one of each of these kind of serpents had appeared in your Council, crushing and poisoning your bishops, would your swallowing an antidote have saved their lives. Alas! no! You can never counteract the serpent's deadly sting, nor have you the power to destroy the sinful desires of the world, the flesh and the Devil, with which every human being is possessed. Nothing but the grace of God can do this. Christ alone can bruise the serpent's head. All that man can do with the help of God's Holy Spirit, is to bruise his heel. St. John warns us of this. In his First Epistle he addresses us as little children, iii. 7, and shows us that, by being righteous alone can we bruise the serpent's heel. The Son of God was manifested to destroy the works of the Devil, but he only acts when we do our part; for it does not say that Christ will bruise his head unless we bruise his heel; here is faith and works.

But if the works of the patriarchs, who had a living faith was imperfect, how can any pope or prelate in these days be infallible? For the first revelation after the fall Christ appeared to man as an angel, and talked with him, and this was not enough to prevent the world from growing gradually more and more wicked. In proof of this assertion, look at the world at the time of the flood. To rest on the seventh day seems to have been the principal command, and, at that time there was but one righteous man found on the earth, who was Noah, who God saved with his family in an *ark*, a word of three letters, which was really the first Church of God on earth. Noah's first act after the flood was to build an altar and offer a sacrifice to God, which showed his faith in a coming Saviour, for which faith he was saved when all the world was drowned; but, though God accepted the offering, he must have seen some imperfection in it, for God said, "I will not curse the ground any more, for the imagination of man's heart is only evil continually." And though he had been so wonderfully preserved, see how soon we read of his being drunken, and he was not infallible enough to keep his three sons in the paths of virtue and holiness, for he was obliged to curse his son Ham for his wickedness; and the next account we have of the world is that pride raged so that man thought he could raise a tower that would reach to heaven, but God frustrated their design by confounding their language, and thus people were scattered over the earth. With a variety of language sprung up, most likely, a variety of false worship. For Abraham was commanded by God himself to remove from the place in which he was living and he would bless him. How sweetly Abraham obeys, old as he was. Seventy-five years of his life he had lived there. He must have had many friends and strong inducements to remain and disobey God; but we hear of no murmur; still he was not infallible. In offering up his son he showed a perfect faith and trust in God's promise of a Messiah, but the poison of the serpent was in his veins, and with him as with all mankind except Christ, the Devil had his hours of triumph. But this is his kingdom, for we know that he is the God of this world, therefore he uses all his arts to allure us, and as long as we live on this earth we must either put on the whole armour of God and fight a daily battle with Satan, or our feet will slide into some bye-path, and we will be overwhelmed by the pomps and vanities of the world. Thus, up to Noah's time, there was no infallible person found on this earth. Noah built, as it were in a figure, the first church. Abraham, in his offering his son, showed us the kind of faith that God requires of us, which must be a willingness to give up the dearest *idol* of our hearts. Isaac's purity and willingness to be offered a perfect type of Christ's love to man. God could have saved Noah without making him build an ark, but God's plan is to make man shew his faith by his works. In building the ark Noah worked out his faith. God might, if He had chosen, have banished sin from this world by Christ's death; but, instead, he has left ordinances and commands to be observed, and a church or ark to carry us through the waters of strife, and to teach us how to escape the snares and nets which the Devil has set to catch us in. Let us look, then, to see that our ark shall be 450 feet long, 75 broad and 45 high, or in other words, that it shall be built as near as possible on the foundation of the Apostles. Jesus Christ himself, " like the figure 5 in the ark," being the chief " corner stone."

"This is the stone which was set at nought of you builders, which is become the head of the corner." Neither is there salvation in any other, for there is none other name under heaven given among men whereby we must be saved. Acts iv. 11, 12., for Christ alone is infallible. If we next take Isaac, we see in the strife and struggling between his sons that he was not infallible, and if Esau, selling his birthright to Jacob, is a type of the Jews rejecting Christ and the call of the Gentiles, the latter part of the blessing, that he shall break the yoke of his neck, will be fulfilled as soon as they acknowledge Christ; for the Jews may be the descendants of Esau and the Christians of Jacob, and the elder in this case have really served the younger. And we have really seen the Scriptures literally fulfilled without perceiving it. We next have the beautiful character of Joseph presented to us. Isaac appears to have been the type of the divine nature of Christ, but Joseph the type of his human nature. See how he is betrayed by his brethren, and sold; see how the Devil tempted him, and see how, guided by God's Holy Spirit, he overcame every temptation, and how beautifully the first revelation of God to man closes with his death. In all the Bible these are the only two characters who did not fail themselves in fulfilling the moral law, but they were not infallible; for their descendants rebelled against their Maker. So loving, good and holy is God, that He now gave man a written law, written with His own finger on two tables of stone; a true picture of the way the Holy Spirit tries to write on our stony hearts, and to transmit these commandments to us—God raised up Moses, a man who God led himself for forty years through many great trials to subdue his angry spirit, and to prepare him for the work which God gave him to do. And now, having found nothing infallible under the first revelation, let us glance at the second, one which was a written revelation, and was given by God himself to Moses, who, after being brought up in the king's palace, is reduced to the occupation of keeping sheep, where he learnt, no doubt, patience and contentment; and the first thing that God tells him is that he is the God of Abraham, Isaac and Jacob. This seems to have been intended for an assurance to Moses that they still existed in some unseen place, for had they altogether passed out of existence God would have said, "I was." Then the bush appearing to be burning without fire to kindle it, was an emblem of the devices which Satan would use to destroy the Church of God; but, kept by God's especial care and purified by God's Holy Spirit, it will, like the ark, when it came through the waters of the flood, cast out all unclean animals which were in it, which animals may, perhaps, be a type of all the different religions and sects which seem, as it were, to have divided the law of Moses between them, to have made four parts of Christ's garments and broken the wedding ring with which Christ had encircled his Church. But the Holy Spirit is coming to open the eyes of the world, and he will bind with faith, hope and charity, the Church in which raging fires have burnt, but which have not destroyed the garments which are prepared for the Bride when she is reunited to her Spouse. Before God gave Moses His written law He talked with him, but, even while God is talking with him he shrinks from the work which was his privilege to perform, forgetting that God would help him, with his Holy Spirit, to do all the work that He gave him to do, provided that he prayed for that help; so God assures him of this help, for He said to him, "Certainly I will be with thee." God chose him as His servant because he had faith in a coming Saviour, and then teaches him that the Holy Spirit would lead him, as he led our Saviour to the wilderness, to endure temptation for us and conquer sin. So the Holy Spirit leads every baptized Christian to try and overcome the sinful desires of the flesh, and, instead, to plant the Christian graces, which St. Paul tells us, are the fruits of the Spirit.

Pharaoh's heart is only a true picture of a man's heart at any time when under the dominion of the Evil Spirit. The ten plagues being one for each commandment that he breaks, and when, by degrees, he thinks nothing of breaking all, preparing himself for endless misery. The first plague, the turning the river Nile into blood, was, there was no doubt, intended to show the Egyptians and Israelites that man must worship the one Holy and true God. The plagues of frogs, lice, flies and beasts, may be a picture of our four religions in the sight of God, when man places his trust in them, instead of being led by God's Holy Spirit to practice the graces which he loves. The plague of boils and blains, of hail, of locusts and thick darkness, a picture of the spiritua state of each of these religions, bound with the sins with which the Devil blinds men's eyes, and the state of corruption which sin has brought our bodies to. Then the last plague teaches us that when we have humbled ourselves to see to what a condition sin has brought us and how soiled and stained our souls are, that there is one perfect sacrifice provided, which alone can wash and purify and fit us to see God; but common sense will tell us that, unless we are led through this world or wilderness by God's Holy Spirit, we will be fit only to be drowned like the Egyptians in the Red Sea, and banished with the wicked from the presence of God. The last plague with which God visited Pharoah was death, and even this heavy calamity did not teach Pharoah to humble himself before God, yet, why so surprised at this, we see coffins and hearses every day, taking to their last home some pilgrims, and how little do we think of it as a lesson which ought to teach us " to do justly, to love mercy, and to walk humbly with thy God."— Micah vi. 8. The great lesson which was foreshadowed by this plague was the death of Christ. God required an atonement for the sins of men, and the Jews were required to offer a lamb from that day till Christ suffered the shameful death of the cross, and offered himself a sacrifice for the sins of the whole world. The command to strike the two side-posts and the upper door-post, is, to my mind, a shadow of the cross, at all events, there were to be the three marks of blood on every Israelite's door; and they were never to fail to keep the Passover as long as they lived. Since Christ's resurrection our Easter has taken its place, and Christians should, with love sincere and holy, pray that God's Holy Spirit would lead them to approach the Lord's table at this sacred time and spiritually to partake of Christ's body and blood, which alone can take the serpent's poison out of our veins. "For there is one God and one Mediator between God and man, the Man Christ Jesus." The Jews were ordered to keep the lamb four days. Now these four days may be a type of the four religions, Jew, Christian, Mahommedan and Brahmin, which, divided as they are now, are keeping us from knowing Christ; but when they unite and form that one tree which man lost when Adam fell, will produce nothing but good fruit, for there will then be no envy, no malice, no striving who will be the greatest, but all will seek to show forth God's glory by their thoughts, words and deeds; there will no more be a constant striving for money, "the love of which is the root of all evil;" but the Christian graces of faith, hope and charity will so fill the hearts and souls of all the world, that earth will become a heaven below, and "the angel having the key of the bottomless pit and a great chain in his hand, will lay hold on the old Serpent, which is the Devil and Satan, and bind him a thousand years." Revelations xx. 1, 2, 3.

The ten dreadful plagues, having so little effect on Pharoah's heart, should teach us to examine closely our own hearts, to see whether our trials and troubles are making us humble and Christ-like, or whether, like Pharoah, we are unwilling to allow our sins to depart from us, but follow them up day by day, till at last they hurry us into everlasting misery. Thinking, like Pharoah, that we are infallible, and wishing the world to worship *us*, instead of our trying to teach the world to worship Christ, by our amiable and gentle ways. For Christians should now try all in their power to lift the cloud from the tabernacle, which keeps the Jew from knowing Christ; and should themselves try and see the pillar of fire, which is God's Holy Spirit, guiding, guarding and leading them to a knowledge of the truth. But, alas! how many will only know him too late! The Holy Spirit has been striving with man ever since the fall, but we know that he has said, in Genesis vi. 3, "My Spirit shall not always strive with man." God will not always strive to see if man will follow the guidance of the Good Spirit, instead of the Evil, and weigh the world and its attractions at their real value. Since the fall of man, God seems to have spoken only five times to man by his Holy Spirit, in a voice that could be heard by mortal ears, besides those two wonderful revelations to Moses in the giving of the Law.* First, in Genesis xvii. 1, God spoke to Abraham, "I am the Almighty God, walk before me and be thou perfect;" and Abraham fell on his face. Twice to Moses; first, in Exodus, iii. 6, "I am the God of thy father, the God of Abraham, the God of Isaac, and the God of Jacob; and Moses fell on his face." In Exodus xxxiii. 20 and following verses, where God tells Moses that no man can see Him and live. In the 18th John, 6th verse, where Jesus says, "I am He;" the divine nature must have spoken, for they went backward and fell to the ground. Then the 17th Matthew, 5 verse: This is my beloved Son, in whom I am well pleased; hear ye Him." Making in all seven times.

Man does not realize the mercy and goodness of God in sending us a written law and begging and

---

* Still in dream and vision it has been heard.

beseeching us by the gentle pleadings of his Holy Spirit to accept salvation now, through the Saviour so that when He comes as King, in a cloud with great glory, we may be able to look up to Him and feel that our redemption draweth nigh. Luke xxi. 27.

Before I close this letter, which I have already spun out to a great length, I wish to call your attention to one fact more, viz.: in the 7th Exodus, 6, "The Lord said to Moses, Aaron thy brother shall be my prophet." Now this is the second priest of which there is any mention, Jethro, Moses' father-in-law, was the first Priest. Moses was a law-giver but not a priest. But in every case the Lord speaks to Moses first. The Jewish law was so intricate, and so minute, that it was impossible to keep it perfectly, "and without shedding of blood is no remission." Hebrews ix. 22. How thankful we should be that the shadow or the cloud has been lifted off our tabernacle, and that the glorious light of the Gospel shows us Christ, the end of the law for righteousness.

"For the law maketh men high priests which have infirmity; but the word of the oath, which was since the law, maketh the Son which is consecrated for evermore." Hebrews vii. 28. Was Aaron, the first high priest, infallible? No. His pride was his destruction. When the people murmured for water in the desert of Zin, Moses and Aaron spoke as if they must fetch the water themselves, (Numbers xx. 10,) forgetting to give the glory of the miracle to God, and for this great sin Aaron was made to mount up to Mount Hor, to be stripped of his garments and to be gathered to his fathers; and, although Moses was allowed to live a little longer, yet, for this same sin he was not allowed to enter into the promised land. Deuteronomy xxxii. 51. Now, allow me to tell your Holiness that, in calling yourself infallible, you have committed exactly the same sin that Moses and

Aaron did at the waters of Meribah-Kadesh, in the wilderness of Zin; and I beseech you, before you are called to appear before your Maker, to retract this dogma which you have just caused to be passed; for, if God punished so heavily those who lived under the law, (Hebrews x. 28, 29,) "Of how much sorer punishment, suppose ye, shall he be thought worthy, who hath trodden under foot the Son of God, and hath counted the Blood of the Covenant, wherewith he was sanctified, an unholy thing, and hath done despite unto the Spirit of Grace." Ponder these things, and may God, in his great mercy, bring you to a knowledge of the sinfulness of all mankind, and the madness of thinking any one infallible. "For all havd sinned and come short of the glory of God."— Romans iii. 23.

THE CHRISTIAN'S ARK.

As vessels point to North or South,
   Or turn their sides to East and West;
So souls of men, by word of mouth,
   Are veering round and seeking rest.

As the needle moves those tiny hands,
   That guides the sailor on his way,
And carries the ship to other lands,
   So do our souls require a stay.

The church of God that stay should be;
   But man has rent and torn it so,
A Christian must become a bee,
   And gather honey to and fro.

A broken cistern it is now,
   Various streams do from it flow;
When we together all do bow,
   One ark again will save from woe.

The ship ere it is fit for sea,
　Is made secure and water-tight,
The rudder must be firm and free,
　The anchor chain hung well in sight.

The compass without the needle's point
　Would dash the ship against the rock;
The word of God must be the joint,
　Christ the anchor, our souls to lock.

Let us pray for the spirit's aid,
　To re-unite with love's cement,
The Church for which Christ's blood was paid,
　And which his death with light'ning rent.

THE EPIPHANY.

　Jesus, prophet, priest and king,
　To thy feet the Magi bring
　Gold and frankincense and myrrh,
　Guided by the heav'nly star.

　Rachel weeping and in pain,
　For her babes by Herod slain;
　All announce the great event,
　The birth of one from heav'n sent.

　Behold him a little child
　Circumcised though free from guile;
　Angels always watching near,
　Name him Jesus, Saviour dear.

　To the Baptist he did go,
　At the river Jordan lo!
　The spirit flew like a dove,
　Resting on him from above.

A voice was heard from the sky,
Manifesting from on high,
That God's own beloved Son,
His first work on earth had done.

Light in triple hue descends,
Threefold blessings man attends;
When we walk, as in God's sight,
The dove will on us alight.

THOUGHTS ON GOOD FRIDAY.

See the Saviour bound and led
   To an earthly judgment seat;
There to hear his sentence read,
   False accusers there to meet.

Judas, his disciple had
   For his idol him betray'd;
Now, we see him very sad,
   For the snare which he had laid.

Jesus always gentle, mild,
   Answers not a single word;
That great crowd, though almost wild,
   Have no word against him heard.

All they can accuse him of,
   That he said he was their King;
So for this they rail and scoff,
   And their insults at him fling.

On his brow a crown of thorns,
   In his hand they put a reed,
Then they take him to be scourg'd;
   Yes, and glory in the deed.

With one loud and piercing cry,
   His Spirit he yielded up;
Sinners think upon that sigh,
   And that dreadful bitter cup.

'Mid two thieves upon the cross,
   The Saviour's body hung;
O, at what a fearful cost,
   Redemption's work was done.

Darkness suddenly appear'd,
   The veil of the temple rent;
Man's heart must indeed be sear'd,
   If such love is vainly spent.

With no selfish end to gain,
   Unlike any other man;
Died to wash away sin's stain,
   Look and all " Behold the Lamb,"

Who has bruis'd the serpent's head,
   Brought both peace and truth to light,
For our souls his blood he shed,
   From the grave return'd with might.

Was he not the greatest King
   That the earth has ever seen;
Should we not together sing,
   Come again, thou glorious beam.

Come with all thy pow'r divine,
   And gather thy scatter'd flock,
With thy arms our souls entwine,
   At our hearts, Lord quickly knock.

ON OUR LENTEN AND OTHER FASTS.

All have some peculiar way
In which they bid you fast and pray,
The Jews did both these things perform,
At stated times they all did mourn.

Samuel did a fast ordain
When going forth the ark to claim,
And offer'd, for a sacrifice,
A lamb, whose incense did arise;

And reach'd Jehovah's mighty throne,
Which in thunderings he made known;
He then the Philistines did smite,
Discomfited, and put to flight.

Even King Ahab, it does say,
Once mourn'd in sackcloth and did pray
That God would him in mercy spare,
And God acceded to his prayer.

Ezra, too, does with fasting plead,
And God did to his wish accede,
He led him safely through the land
Where danger lurk'd on ev'ry hand.

When Nehemiah did desire
The Jewish people to inspire
With courage, to rebuild their walls,
With fasting on his knees he falls.

A gracious answer God did send,
The people did to him attend,
And round the city did appear
The walls, which he work'd hard to rear.

The King of Nineveh, when sad,
In sackcloth did his people clad,
They mourn'd, they fasted, and they pray'd,
And the destroying angel stay'd.

Priests, ministers, and elders, all
Joel did gather at his call,
A fast he then did sanctify,—
From God's own house they sent their cry.

But fasting may be made a snare,
Isaiah says of this beware,
If done with strife or with debate,
With sin such fasting will checkmate.

Christians, we have much to fear,
For it is really plain and clear
That we in concert never fast,
Nor are our prayers in one mould cast.

Five feasts the Jewish people held,
Or from communion were expell'd;
No such rules do Christians mind,
So Satan scores of them do bind.

It thus behoves us all to see
The reasons why we disagree,
Together we must sift our creeds
Ere they are chok'd with Satan's weeds.

The tares, now sown among the wheat,
We must tread down beneath our feet;
All pride and prejudice must bend,
Our ways and works we must amend.

God's truth will plainly then appear,
His voice again we all shall hear,
The chaff will quickly fly away
When Christians all together pray.

Christ said himself he was the way,
Truth he did faithfully portray;
When his example does us guide
From virtue we will never slide.

First, see him as a little child—
Obedient, loving, meek and mild,
In wisdom he did daily grow,
Which he afterwards did show.

At twelve years old he did men teach
To use the means within their reach,
For see him at the Jewish feast,
Preparing for the work of Priest.

For seventeen or eighteen years
No record of his life appears,
P'raps, in the quiet of his home,
He like a star of beauty shone.

When nearly thirty years of age
In his great work he does engage,—
To carry out God's great design
His body he did then resign.

We first perceive he was baptiz'd,
Though he before was circumcis'd,
The spirit on him like a dove,
Show'd a father's special love.

The Baptist said he was the Lamb,
The one great substitute for man,
Completely pure and free from guile,
No spot or blemish did defile.

Then see the Tempter plied his arts,
And tried to pierce him with his darts,
When in the desert weary, lone,
He his long fasting did make known.

Like Moses and Elias, he
For forty days did fast, we see,
This is the origin of Lent,
Why then should some from it dissent.

It must be the various ways
Christians keep these forty days,
Have made it one of Satan's snares,
His harvest time for sowing tares.

Christ bid us heed no vain command,
His word to hear and understand,
Not that which goeth in defiles,
But that which cometh out beguiles.

All evil from the heart proceeds,
That is the source of wicked deeds;
Both fish and flesh life will sustain
When truth flows freely through each vein.

We cannot fast when we eat fish
For it is quite a dainty dish,
Besides, the multitude Christ fed
With bread and fish, St. Matthew said;

Lest fasting they should faint away,
As they did journey on the way;
Christ, like a kind and thoughtful friend,
From unseen dangers did defend.

He knew well ere they reached their homes
Satan would feed them with his stones,
If hungry they from him did go
Surrounded they would be with woe.

The Esquimaux on fish subsist,
Without it how can they exist?
If eating fish is call'd a fast
Their fasting days for ever last.

No rules for fasting do we find
In Holy Writ for us combined,
Our blessed Lord's example though
Its great necessity does show.

To keep our bodies in control,
To fix our thoughts upon the soul,
From earthly trifles to retire,
And gather up some Holy Fire.

Each one knows best the tempting thing
That daily leads him on to sin,
If it for forty days we curb,
The still small voice would so disturb—

That Satan would relax his hold,
And we could drive him from the fold,
The Bride, her jewels would display,
For we would walk in wisdom's way.

When we keep fast days as we should
God will give us heavenly food,
Such as the Jews for forty years
Did gather daily it appears.

Their murmurings and discontent
Its hidden virtue did prevent—
From shedding all its light around,
It only sparkled on the ground.

But when we all united try
Our souls to feed from God on high,
The golden manna God will show'r,
And Christ will come again with pow'r.

As the Messiah, King of kings,
He comes with healing in his wings;
Then those on earth will reappear
Whose worship was to him sincere

Who Satan never did betray
Their homage to his gold to pay;
But, with the blessings God did give,
Taught other people how to live.

Our fasting days will then bear fruit,
And angels will our ranks recruit;
New joys will then our souls entrance,
Our minds with knowledge will advance.

Nations of every shade and hue
Will give to God what is his due;
Man then will cease to be perverse,
And God will from us take the curse.

THE TRANSFIGURATION.

Jesus, Peter, James and John,
   Went upon a mountain high,
Jesus' face shone as the sun,
   Transfigur'd before their eye.

With him other two were seen,
   Moses and Elias call'd;
What a wondrous, dazzling scene;
   But still they were not appall'd.

Their appearance seems to say,
   In him the Messiah see,
We rejoice to see his day,
   For he soon will set us free.

Peter always earnest spake,
   Thought the place they must revere;
Ask'd to be allow'd to make,
   Tabernacles three. Lo! Hear

A voice suddenly disturbs
   Them from this, their great design,
They are startled by the words:
   This beloved Son is mine.

The Shekinah then was seen,
   Drawing them beneath his wing;
Giving forth a little gleam,
   Of the great and mighty king.

For whose glory they should use,
   All their energy and skill;
Human idols all refuse,
   And alone perform his will.

Not build tabernacles three;
   But unite, and all in one,
To Jehovah bend the knee,
   With the Spirit through the Son.

MARK XIII.

Andrew, Peter, James and John
   Asked Jesus for a sign,
Which they could depend upon,
   And that all might know the time

When the temple would be chang'd,
   When its grandeur all would fade;
All its very stones derang'd,
   As he then to them had said.

Take heed and let none deceive,
   Many in my name shall come;
And some work they will achieve
   Before evil's race is run.

Famine, earthquakes, trouble, war,
   Must needs be before the end;
Christian sorrows near and far,
   These events will all portend.

That Christ's second advent's near,
  In the clouds with glory great,
Suddenly he will appear,
  His elect to reinstate.

That day and hour none doth know,
  'Tis the great Creator's will,
That his creatures here below,
  Must first, all his work fulfil.

'Till then we must watch and pray;
  Keeping faithful to the end,
Making Christ our hope and stay,
  Loving him, the sinner's friend.

THE SPIRIT LAND.

Three days Christ with the spirit dwelt,
  When his work on earth was done,
What joy the Fathers must have felt
  When their spirits saw God's Son.

St. Peter tells us that Christ preach'd
  To them in their prison gates;
He does not say that he could reach
  Beyond to a future state.

Nothing but pow'r divine could soar
  To that far off spirit-land;
Unreach'd by any human lore,
  Or chang'd by a priestly hand.

The sting of Death Christ did destroy,
  Its gates he will soon unchain;
Then saints and prophets he'll employ,
  His sacrifice to sustain.

When sin is bound and goodness reigns,
  Jerusalem will descend,
Then earth will no more groan with pain,
  For Babylon's reign will end.

THE SACRAMENTS.

A Sacrament, what does it mean,
Food to strengthen and make clean;
To purge from sin and make quite whole,
Not the body, but the soul.

On this great point men now contend,
All do their belief defend,
With what they find in Holy Writ,
Which in pieces must be split.

For some say that there are but two,
Some insist you seven should do;
Others allow there may be three,
Search, and five you there shall see.

Five means whereby our souls may feed,
All which to the altar lead;
The place where once Jehovah dwelt,
Where the Jewish people knelt.

All the five books that Moses wrote,
And which all do read and quote;
Teach that our Maker did provide,
Food for body, soul and mind.

Five animals did Abram slay,
Upon that eventful day;
When the Lord met him in disguise,
To accept his sacrifice

He with him then a cov'nant seal'd,
To his spirit then reveal'd;
Blessings his seed should yet acquire,
Signing it with Holy Fire.

This Abram did such faith display,
That the Lord again did say;
All nations shall through thee be bless'd,
Thus he this to him exprest.

Then, we are told in after years,
The Lord once more to him appears;
His former covenant renew'd,
With new grace this man endu'd.

Which grace to all his seed would flow,
If their faith they all did show,
By circumcising every male.
Still this custom does prevail

Among the Jews who claim to be,
Abram's sole posterity;
But Christians also this may claim,
Though their faith has chang'd their name.

'Tis true, they do not circumcise,
But instead, they do baptize;
From this old law Christ set us free,
With his perfect purity.

It may be, both of these may trace
Their various means of grace
To the two sons, who once did cheer
Abram in his sojourn here.

Both of these lads their God did fear,
And his angel's voice did hear,
Promising blessings on their seed,
Manifold, and great indeed.

N

Isaac, Abraham's son and heir,
To bless Esau did prepare;
When Jacob, by his mother told,
His poor brother Esau sold.

On account of Rebekah's sin,
Jacob did the birthright win;
But Esau's sons will yet embrace
Much more perfect means of grace.

For his mother's deceitful sway
Open'd to Esau's sons the way
To be earth's great beacon light,
And regain their lost birthright.

When at the cross they lowly bend,
The great strife on earth will end;
Our yoke of sin will quickly fall,
When Christ is our all in all.

Then, producing a perfect ark,
Lit up with a heavenly spark;
The grapes that Christ on earth did plant,
Will together sing and chant.

And with five sacramental cords,
Will await the Lord of lords;
For his miracles all do show,
His great love through them must flow.

Five virgins in the days of old,
Sybils call'd, of Christ foretold;
These prophesied that he was near,
As they said he did appear.

Christ was the long expected star,
Who with Satan did wage war;
The battle which he did proclaim,
Christians ever since maintain.

A sword, he said, he with him brought,
Which he, his disciples taught;
Would all the ties of home divide,
Discord spread on ev'ry side.

Blood from his side, his hands, his feet,
Made his sacrifice complete;
Five were the wounds Christ did endure,
The disease of sin to cure.

A type each wound must surely be,
On this point we must agree;
Five means of grace we must embrace,
Ere we christianise the race.

When Christians altogether cleave,
Miracles they will achieve;
Bethesdas' waters then will heal,
Christ their virtues will reveal.

Through its five porches all the meek
Proper remedies will seek,
And those who now are deaf and blind,
Sight and hearing both will find.

We will not then be forc'd to wait,
Or recline at mercy's gate,
The Sun of Righteousness will shine,
Proving that he is Divine.

Five loaves of bread did Jesus take,
And among five thousand break,
Enough they had, and some to spare,
Fragments, we are told there were.

Two fishes with the bread they ate,
Emblem of the life we get,
When at the altar we do kneel,
And our faith with works do seal.

Five virgins with five lamps of oil,
Well prepar'd with care and toil,
The Bridegroom when he comes to meet,
By his side will take their seat.

First, with water Christian born,
Virtues graces to adorn;
The sponsor vows in infant's name,
To avoid both sin and shame.

When the child has reach'd his teens,
He should use himself the means
For taking up those vows again,
Using ev'ry link of chain

That binds us to the Christian name,
Keeps alive the holy flame:
We then may drink the bread and wine,
Fountain of the living vine.

With Christ's blood new life is giv'n,
To destroy all sin and leaven;
Our souls renew'd with heav'nly grace,
Joy and happiness will taste.

Then, when Adam his Eve does find,
God's own sacrament will bind;
Great blessings will on them descend,
Love will ev'ry home attend.

Then all those foolish, flirting ways,
In which people pass their days,
Will not, as now, engender strife,
Poisoning the joys of life.

Money will not be so ador'd,
Minds with other wealth be stor'd;
The golden rays our God will send,
Will our thoughts and ways amend.

Life will then, as before the flood,
Yield a stronger, purer blood;
Hundreds of years will find us bright,
Ears not deaf, nor dull our sight.

All the priests who perform these rites,
Will be pure and clothed in white;
The breast-plate then again will show
Twelve bright jewels in a row.

When taking ordination vows,
Bishop's hands upon their brows,
The glory of the Lord will shine,
And around these jewels twine.

Then God will us absolve from sin,
Making us quite pure within;
His presence will our path surround,
And Heav'n will on earth be found.

ACTS XVII. 18.

When Paul in the midst of Mars' Hill did stand,
The people of Athens to reprimand,
An altar to the unknown God he found,
And ignorant worshippers all around.

These were a people who thought themselves wise,
And gaily, embark'd with great enterprise
In all worldly schemes their country to raise;
But Paul found it hard to teach them God's ways.

He reason'd and argued, they only mock'd,
What, part with their idols! this was a shock;
They call'd him a babbler, and thought him mad,—
In a vision the Lord said, be not sad,

And hold not thy peace, for I am with thee,
But take courage poor soul and patient be,
Some of my people this city contains,
Whose love for me freely flows through their veins.

When all selfish thoughts they begin to crush,
And all evil transactions from them thrust,
Their spiritual eyesight will return,
And right from wrong they will plainly discern.

THE ST. PATRICK.

One of the Allen Steamers as seen May, 1873, when she keeled over in the Dock.

A vessel on her side we see,
   St. Patrick is her name,
She in a moment over-keeled
   And a sad wreck became.

Many times she the Ocean crossed,
   With safety and with pride,
The tempest often did her toss,
   Still bravely did she glide.

But yet within the harbor docks
   When ready all to sail,
The rudder all their efforts mocks
   Until she meets the gale.

Then water masters gains control,
   Her cargo melts away,
Divers are sought to close all holes,
   And fill with tow each stay.

Three engines fast to her are made,
   Much water out they pump,
But still *St. Patrick* firm is staid,
   She rests where first she sunk.

When first the steamer fell, the mast
    With stick across did keep,
Until they tied and made her fast,
    Where now she seems to sleep.

The Christian Church must now awake
    And trim her sails anew,
For God's own spirit soon will rake
    And influence the Jew

To open out his Temple Gate,
    And plant within the Cross,
Christians then will find it late,
    To clear away the dross,

And make it Christ-like to behold,
    Cemented well with love,
Containing nought but purest gold
    And gentle cooing doves.

It should be like a beacon light,
    Emitting such a blaze,
That all must keep it in their sight,
    And feel its piercing rays.

All there should find good Holy Oil,
    Themselves the lamps to fill,
The Tempter's Arts we then should foil,
    And do our Maker's will.

It is so much divided now,
    The rudder cannot work,
So when the Jew begins to plough,
    And wakens up the Turk,

She will I fear receive a shock,
    Which will her paralyse,
And will, just like this ship in dock,
    Sink down before our eyes.

THIS SCROLL
IS ADDRESSED TO THE
ARCHIBISHOP OF SYRA AND TENOS,

MOST ILLUSTRIOUS PATRIARCH.

This letter which I once addressed you on Christian unity I am about to array in new and more costly robes, and to entwine around it others which at various times the Holy Spirit has moved me to write. In its new and improved condition I trust that it may be the means of inducing your branch of the Christian Church to have a careful investigation of its leading doctrines, and if when well weighed in a just balance they are found wanting, to make an effort to regain the treasures lost, that instead of protesting against each other, as Christians have been doing for centuries, we may become such a united tower of strength that all the Devil's schemes will fall before our great uplifted arm. Nothing but this can stay the growth of infidelity, which is spreading itself like the fangs of a great cancer all through the earth.

The greatest sin of the world in the present day seems to be a want of knowledge of the person and work of the Holy Spirit. How little is the creed of St. Athanasius understood! men talk of the great advancement that this age has made in civilization, but, alas! has either Synod or Council, lately met, produced anything in any way to compete with it? A great part of mankind seems to understand the great work of God the Son, but few, very few, ever consider the patience, long suffering and ever active work of God the Holy Ghost; but as St. Mark has warned us, that to blaspheme against the Holy Ghost has never forgiveness, it behoves us well to consider the work of the Spirit of God, which alone enables us to contend with the Evil Spirit; God the Father made the world and man, and pronounced it a finished work; God the Son redeemed the whole human race, with the price of blood—this is also a finished work—but God the Holy Ghost's work is a progressive work, it is to continue till at last man, through his influence, will become the pure and holy being he was made at first. As soon as man strives to be holy, those thousand years will begin which are spoken of in the 20th chapter of Revelations, for it is evident, that the time spoken of there, is a time when goodness is to abound on the earth, and to restore it to its original beauty. David's prayer in Psalm li. 2, "And take not thy Holy Spirit from me," shews us that David found himself unable to contend with the powers of darkness without the Divine aid. Isaiah says, "But they rebelled and vexed his Holy Spirit." "Where is he that put his holy spirit within him?"—lxiii. 10, 11. These passages shew that God's Holy Spirit is a person engaged in a warfare with the Evil Spirit. Turning to the New Testament St. Luke tells us xi. 13, "How much more shall your Heavenly Father give the Holy Spirit to them that ask him." Ephes. i. 13, "In whom also after that ye believed ye were sealed with that Holy Spirit of Promise." Eph. iv. 30 warns us "Grieve not the Holy Spirit of God." 1st Thes. iv. 8, "Who hath also given unto us his Holy Spirit." These passages, three from the Old, and four from the New Testament, prove the beautiful words of the creed, "the Godhead of the Father, of the Son, and of the Holy Ghost, is all one, the glory equal, the Majesty co-eternal."

God the Holy Ghost is speaking to man now in fire, wind, earthquakes, pestilence and war, imploring them to worship and serve the great Creator and to become temples fit for the habitation of the Holy Spirit. God the Father gave man ten commandments, and sent priests and prophets to teach men how to keep them, but as these all failed to keep them themselves, God sent his own Son to shew the world, by a practical life, the beauty of holiness, and by his death to ransom the souls of those who, through the help of God's Holy Spirit, overcame the world.

God has made seven promises to those that overcome the temptations of the Evil one in the world. 1. "To him that overcometh will I give to eat of the Tree of life, which is in the midst of the Paradise of God."—Rev. ii. 7. The one that eats of that tree will never die, for we are told in Gen. iii. 22, that Adam was driven out of Paradise to prevent him from eating of this tree which would enable him to live for ever. 2nd. "He that overcometh shall not be hurt of the second death." He who has the privilege of living on this earth with a glorified body when the Holy Spirit reigns as King will also rise to glory when Christ comes as a judge. 3rd. "To him that overcometh will I give to eat of the hidden manna, and will give him a white stone, and in the stone a new name written which no man knoweth saving he that receiveth it."—Rev. ii. 17. 4th. "He that overcometh and keepeth my words unto the end to him will I give power over the nations."—*Ibid.* 26th verse. 5th. "He that overcometh the same shall be clothed in white raiment, and I will not blot out his name out of the Book of Life, but I will confess his name before my Father, and before his Angels.—Rev. iii. 5. 6th. "Him that overcometh will I make a pillar in the Temple of my God: and he shall go no more out: and I will write upon him the name of my God and the name of the city of my God, which is New Jerusalem, which cometh down out of heaven from my God; and I will write upon him my new name."—Rev. iii. 12. 7th. "Him that overcometh will I grant to sit with me in my throne, even as I also overcame, and am set down with my Father in his throne."—iii. 21. And besides all this the 21st Rev., 7th verse, says, "He that overcometh shall inherit all things, and I will be his God and he shall be my Son."

O, could man but recognize the blessings which are in store for those that resist the Devil, and his temptations, the state to which they would restore the world, if there was one united effort to become practically good, not as it is now, to be very careful to keep one or two of the commandments because man's laws would expose and punish them if they break them, but to keep God's day holy out of love, reverence and fear to the Great and Almighty God, and then to act towards man after the example of our blessed Saviour, would make this earth a heaven below. God never gave commandments that man had not the power to obey; with these commands God gave man his Holy Spirit to keep him in the path of peace and holiness. Baruch says in his Epistle to Jeremy, vi. ch., 60 verse, that sun, moon, and stars being bright and sent to do their offices are obedient, and man alone defies and disobeys his Maker and Creator.

Before giving these commandments God gave to Abraham two sacraments, as means through which spiritual life should be planted, and cherished as it were in the heart of man; "and Melchizedech, king of Salem, brought forth bread and wine: and he was the priest of the most High God, and he blessed Abraham."—Gen. xiv. 18. St. Paul tells us in Heb. vii. that this priest had three names, King of Righteousness, King of Salem and King of Peace, thus teaching Abraham that the God that made, would redeem and glorify a people for himself, who after living on this earth with a glorified body, will become Angels, filling the place of those who had fallen from their first estate. Three chapters after we read of the Lord appearing to Abraham and saying, "I am the Almighty God; walk before me and be thou perfect." Then God established his covenant of circumcision with his faithful Abraham. Thus we see the first thing God gave man after the flood was two sacraments, renewing as it were, the seed of goodness in the heart of man and preparing it for the law which he afterwards gave by the hands of his servant Moses.

Now let us look at the practical way in which our Saviour fulfilled the will of God. When eight days of his life were accomplished Luke tells us in ii. 21, that he was circumcised, and his name Jesus given. Matthew mentions the name, but seems to think it unnecessary to speak of the act of circumcision, thinking, perhaps, that none could doubt it, but gives us instead two names, one for his divine nature, which is Emanuel, or "God with us," and one for his human nature, which is Jesus, by being circumcised after the law and humbly submitting to all things necessary to our salvation. He fulfilled the prophecy in Isaiah xlii. 21, "He will magnify the law and make it honorable." Could he have magnified it unless he had submitted to it? No; in being circumcised he did magnify it. But as Christ took all our sins upon him, and bore all our pains, so he instituted in place of circumcision, baptism, which is as binding on the Christian as circumcision was on the Jew. A Jew was not a Jew unless he was circumcised. A Christian is not a Christian till he is baptized. No stranger could keep the passover unless he had been circumcised—Ex. xii. 48—so no Christian can go to the Lord's table unless he has been baptized, for as soon as the Jews believed on Christ they were baptized. John was circumcised before Christ, Luke i. 59. His baptism is not mentioned, but he is called the Baptist, which evidently means more than is expressed. John seems to have expected that Christ's Baptism would have had a much more powerful effect, and been altogether different from his; but Christ, to make it plain to John that he was only going to fulfil the law not to change it, submits at once to John's Baptism, shewing us, by this act, how necessary it was to salvation, and that the power that he would give his ministers would enable them to make men Christians, to enlist them, as it were, under his banner, just as circumcision made them Jews. As a general rule Christians do not appreciate because they do not know the great privilege of being made a member of Christ, of having the seed of a power planted within them which will enable them successfully to contend with the Spirit of Evil, which daily attacks the souls of men.

To illustrate the subject, without making light of the ordinance of baptism, suppose there was any way in which people might become members of the Royal Family of England, and so be made heirs of their privileges if they strictly obeyed certain laws. How eager all would be to learn the way! no trouble would be spared, no sacrifice thought too great to obtain it. But because Christ's kingdom at present is spiritual, and so not outwardly visible, our faith is cold and dead. There is no doubt that the good rule of baptising children when they are eight days old is the one the Christian Church should begin to try and enforce, one who really believes in the ordinance and the benefits to be received thereby would not be pained by seeing children die without being enrolled among Christ's lambs, and people would not be satisfied to live a great part of their lives, without availing themselves of so glorious a privilege. In Matt. xx. 23, Christ seems to say to the mother of Zebedee's children, while on earth you may have the great privilege of being baptized and partaking of my Holy Supper, but when I come as King, I will place those on my right hand who have loved and obeyed me, but of that you can know nothing now. Matt. xix. 13 shews that Christ blessed little children and put his hands on them. It was not needful that Christ should use water, he could give the spirit without the water; but the water, like the Church, is the channel through which his grace must flow. When Jesus was baptized the Holy Spirit descended in a visible manner, and a voice from heaven declared him to be the Son of God. When we are baptized the Holy Spirit descends in an invisible manner, seen only through the eye of faith. Adam's first act was disobedience; Christ's first act was obedience. Every act of Christ's life shewed forth the glory of God, and every act of men's lives is to glorify themselves.

How simple the means that Christ employs for a test of our faith! the Spirit, the water, and the blood, the three parts of which man is made, thus teaching us that we must give ourselves to God, and live for the glory of the One, who is our Creator, Redeemer and Sanctifier. The work is his own, he will finish it; he will never leave man as he is, degraded by sin and selfishness, but as soon as man puts forth his energies to please and serve him, at the same time trying to subdue himself, he will become one with Christ, and the Holy Spirit will come in person and will reign, then will be heard the great voice saying, "the Kingdoms of this world are become the Kingdoms of our Lord and of his Christ.—Rev. xi. 15.. And he shall reign forever and ever."

The Jews had a mercy seat, an altar of incense and a table made of wood and covered with gold, on which stood twelve cakes of bread with golden dishes and spoons, but none but the Priests were allowed to eat of it, Exodus xxv. Christ having shed his blood for all, commands all to show their faith in him by eating of this bread, "Take, eat, this is my body." It was no longer to remain in the hands of the priests. The twelve apostles were to take it and dispense it to the people together with the wine. "Drink ye all of it, for this is my blood of the New Testament." The Jews had been forbidden to touch blood by God himself, Gen. ix. 4, so that by this command alone he shewed the Jews that Divine wrath was satisfied. The Lamb was slain, the world was redeemed, now priests and people had but to believe and to obey. Then there was a candlestick made of pure gold, like a pillar with three branches on each side, so that it held one lamp on the top, and six lamps on the branches, making altogether seven lights, Ex. xxv. And in Rev. iv. it says, "There were seven lamps of fire burning before the throne, which are the seven spirits of God." Besides these four things which belonged to the most Holy place, there was the altar of burnt offerings, which was five cubits long, made of wood, and overlaid with brass, with shovels, fire-pans, basins and other vessels belonging to it, Ex. xxvii. 1-5. This Altar, like the table of shewbread, is now quite useless. "He taketh away the first that he may establish the second." "By the which will we are sanctified through the offering of the body of Jesus Christ once for all." Heb. x. 9, 10. Then there was the laver, a vessel of brass containing a large quantity of water for the priests to wash their hands and feet in, when they went to do service in the Tabernacle; these two things were kept in the court of the Tabernacle in the open sky. The water and burnt offering represent to my mind the outward form or thing signified in the two principal sacraments which Christ ordained and the light which was within the Holy Place the type of the inward and spiritual grace which is poured out on those who partake of these sacraments in faith.

One thing mankind would do well to consider: the devil did not by his treachery to Adam and Eve succeed in destroying the spirit of man. The beautiful body with which Adam was clothed received within it a poison which caused its death, but the soul, if lost, is lost through the pride and self-will of each individual, for before he had time to finish his work, God said, "I will put enmity between thee and the woman, between thy seed and her seed," interposing, as it were, God's Holy Spirit, in the heart of man, to be a sword by which each creature has a power within himself, a conscience which warns us when we are allowing any temptation to soil our spirit with an impure thought or word or action. Well might St. Paul exclaim, "O the depth of the riches both of the wisdom and knowledge of God. How unsearchable are his judgments and his ways past finding out," but man must never forget, that though he may overcome all the trials and temptations of the world he yet needs to be washed in his Saviour's blood. And to keep this always in our minds, God gave us another sacrament, to nourish and cherish the seed of spiritual life sown in the heart at baptism. By the careful and constant use of this sacrament, goodness grows as it were in the heart of man until he becomes a tree planted by the rivers of waters that bringeth forth his fruit in his season.—Psalm 1. And this tree, after it has *blossomed* here, will be translated to another and brighter sphere, never again to shed its leaves, but to be arrayed in fine linen, pure and white, for the fine linen is the righteousness of the Saints.—Rev. xix. 6.

For the use of these sacraments and for the keeping of the Law God gave man a Priesthood. Jethro was the first human priest mentioned in Scripture, but the term priest is first applied in Genesis xiv. 18. to Melchizedek King of Salem, who brought forth bread and wine, and instituted spiritually the Lord's Supper. The blessing of Abraham seems to have been a type of our ordination service. St. Paul tells us in Heb. vii. 3, that this priest was made like the Son of God, that he had neither beginning of days nor end of life, thus proving himself to be the Holy Spirit of God; he thus appeared spiritually to teach us that a holy man with a good family was a blessing to mankind, that such holy living made him fit to teach the world that it is God's pleasure that the world should worship him first, individually; secondly, that divided into families, they should worship him collectively; and thirdly, that these families should form a church and worship him in a body in spirit and in truth. Now, let me implore you to try every doctrine of the faith of your branch of the Christian Church by the Word of God, and to induce the other churches to do the same, that all may become one candlestick, whose bright and powerful light will draw all men unto it, bringing them to the knowledge and love of the true God, and the temple which was rent in twain at the Saviour's death will be cemented by the cords of love. Peace and holiness will dwell in every heart, and this world will become a Paradise such as Eden was when Adam was placed in it to dress and keep it.

Let us examine and trace the genealogy of the earthly Priesthood. The Priest of Midian, whose name was Reuel, was the son of Bashemath, the wife of Esau.—Gen. xxxvi. 10. Bashemath was one of the daughters of Heth, Gen. xxvii. 46, and Heth, we know, was the son of Canaan, x. 15. So the first priest was descended from the Canaanites. The next thing we know of the Priesthood is that the Levites were set apart for that office. Levi had three sons, Gershom, Kohath, and Merari; Amram was Kohath's eldest son, and he married his father's sister, who was the mother of Moses and Aaron, so that they were Levites, and Moses married the daughter of Reuel, the priest of Midian, who, I have shown you, was a Canaanite. Aaron the High Priest married Elisheba, whose genealogy is not given, except that she was the daughter of Aminadab.—Ex. vi. 23. Aaron had four sons, who were all priests; two of these offered strange fire before the Lord, and they were killed by fire from Heaven, Lev. x. 2. These four priests are now represented in the world by four religions, all of whom have priests. Do none of them offer strange fire before the Lord? it certainly behoves us to see what sort of fire we are offering. Had it been a purifying fire, the result would be such as God requires. Instead of that, when we review the subject, it is evident that God's first great design, which was frustrated by the poison inserted by the devil, was that man should live on this earth, and rule over every living creature and thing which God created in an innocent and happy state. Has this end yet been attained? Has this earth yet become the kingdom of our Lord? Has God's promise to Abraham that "all nations of the earth shall be blessed" yet been fulfilled? if not, may we not hope that God's Holy Spirit will fulfil all this? I have shewn you that as soon as the poison was inserted God gave man a conscience to teach him how he could recover his happy state. When men failed to listen to this still small voice, the flood swept them away. Then the patriarchal age commenced, and with it, faith in the coming Saviour; the Jews were certainly God's chosen people, but why? because they alone, of all the dwellers upon earth, knew the Lord. In the family of Abraham the priesthood had its origin. Abraham, Isaac and Jacob are types, as it were, of the three orders of ministers; but in those days people worshipped the Sun, for we read of Joseph marrying Asenath, the daughter of Potipherah, the priest of On, Gen. xli, 45, so that it is clear that the reason why God loved the Jews was because in the midst of idolatry they loved and worshipped him alone. Then God gave man a written law which is called the beginning of the Levitical age, which had its beginning at Mount Sinai, and was entrusted to the High Priest, Priest and Levite; and which ended in the awful crucifixion and death of the Son of God; and we, having had the benefit of all these privileges, now live under the dispensation of Grace.

The redemption and glorification of this world was the ground work of the Faith of all the Old Testament Saints. Adam beheld it like a star over his dark future. Abraham looked for a "city which hath foundation whose builder and maker is God." Job says "yet in my flesh shall I see God," and looked for the time when "His flesh shall be fresher than a child, he shall return to the days of his youth." David and the four great Prophets describe its future glory. Our blessed Lord and his Apostles shewed by their lives and doctrines the character of those which would realize their fulfilment. How is it that though nineteen centuries have nearly passed since the world was redeemed, it has not yet become glorified? It must be the want of unity among Christians which prevents mankind from having on the whole armour of God, which alone enables him to fight with the devil and prevail against him, which he can do, for

Christ has said, "If a man keep my sayings he shall never see death." "A little while and ye shall not see me, and again a little while and ye shall see me." "I pray not that thou shouldest take them out of the world, but that thou shouldest keep them from the evil."

Observe that the serpent has appeared to man in three forms, first as the serpent when he poisoned the beautiful creature God made; then as Satan, under which name he is said to have resisted David, Job, and Joshua, and to stand at the right hand of all who do wickedly.—Psalm cix. But it was as the devil that he tempted our Saviour. It seems as if it was then that he first came on earth as a man, and though we are told that he is to leave the earth for a time, that is, that he is to be chained, for in Rev. xx. it says that the serpent, the devil, and Satan, the three in one, will be bound and cast into the bottomless pit for a thousand years. Yet the wickedness of the world at present makes it evident that the tempter, the accuser and the deceiver are still here.—"As a roaring lion walketh about seeking whom he may devour, 1st Peter v. 8, and will continue till the Holy Spirit comes to reign on earth. Many times in the Old Testament the people are said to sacrifice to devils, Lev. xvii. 7; Deut. xxxii. 17; Psalm cvi. 37, and in II Chronicles xi., 15, we are told that Jeroboam ordained him Priests for the high places and for the devils. Thus we see that every thing that God has done for the salvation of man, the devil has done to destroy him. God gave Priests, the devil did so too; when Christ appeared spiritually, the devil did so too; when Christ came as a man, the devil clothed himself as a man and appeared on earth. But Christ ascended up to heaven and desired his followers to shew their faith by their works. The devil sets up an idol, the world falls down and worships it. Man was never made to spend his whole life in the pursuit of gold, and yet from youth to age the one thought of men's lives is how shall I make money? When made, how invest it; when invested, how shall I spend it to the most advantage for this perishing body. They hoard it, they worship it, it is the idol of men's hearts. Like the image that Nebuchadnezzar set up, it must be shattered when the stone becomes a great mountain, and fills the whole earth, it will break it to pieces.

Let us look now into the ancient names in the Bible for places set apart for the worship of God. In Exodus xxv. 8, we are told God said to Moses, "Let them make me a sanctuary, that I may dwell among them according to all that I shew thee after the pattern of the Tabernacle." Before this God seemed to have made a place for himself, for in Ex. xv. 17, "In the place, O Lord, which thou hast made for thee to dwell in, in the sanctuary, O Lord, which thy hands have established," and Hebrews viii. 2, says, "A minister of the sanctuary and of the true tabernacle which the Lord pitched and not man." Joshua, just before his death, wrote "in the book of the law of God, and took a great stone and set it up there under an oak, that was by the sanctuary of the Lord," xxiv. 26. God promised Moses that " the tabernacle shall be sanctified by my glory. I will sanctify the tabernacle of the congregation and the altar. I will sanctify also both Aaron and his sons, to minister to me in the Priest's office." Samuel is the first that calls the tabernacle a temple, 1st Saml. i. 9, so that, with prophecy, the name temple seems to have originated. But Solomon was the one chosen to build a temple for the sanctuary, "Take heed now, for the Lord hath chosen thee to build an house for the Sanctuary, be strong and do it."—1 Chronicles xxviii. 10. The tabernacle was moveable; the temple was immoveable. But, when we read of the nineteen wicked kings that reigned over Israel, after they were separated from Judah, and of the idols they set up, we are not surprised that God allowed the temple to be destroyed. Of the twenty kings that reigned over Judah, a few were very religious, some very wicked, and others of an indifferent and mixed character, but so little effect had Solomon's teaching had that in the fifth year of Rehoboam's reign, Shishak, king of Egypt, plundered the temple and the king's house, so soon was it necessary to punish them for their idolatry, which sin seems to have gradually increased among them. Once, indeed, in Hezekiah's reign, we read that many out of several tribes came to the Passover, so that "there was great joy in Jerusalem, for since the time of Solomon, the son of David, king of Israel, there was not the like in Jerusalem."—2 Chro. xxx. 26. Then the good king Josiah repaired the temple and restored the worship of God, and finding a book of the law of the Lord by Moses, he rent his clothes to think how little the law had been observed.—2 Chron. xxxiv. 19. In Chapter xxxv. 18, we are told the Passover that Josiah kept in his reign was even better than king Solomon's, because it was more in conformity to the rules appointed by Moses. In the words of Scripture, "There was no Passover like to that kept in Israel from the days of Samuel the prophet, neither did all the kings of Israel keep such a Passover as Josiah kept and the priests, and the Levites, and all Judah and Israel that were present, and the inhabitants of Jerusalem." But sad, to say he met his death from disobedience, he went to fight with the king of Israel without the direction of God, and was slain.

After his death, the Jews grew more and more wicked till at last the king of Babylon burnt the temple of the Lord, the palace of the king, and all the houses in Jerusalem, carrying away all the vessels of gold, silver and brass, that belonged to the temple. Then, according to the prophecy of Jeremiah, the land was, in some measure, desolate seventy years. (Jer. xxv. 11, 12), until Cyrus, after he took Babylon, gave them leave to rebuild the temple, and restored the vessels of gold and silver to Sheshbazzar, the Prince of Judah, to the number of five thousand four hundred. Ezra i. 11. Thus fulfilling the prophecy made by Isaiah above a hundred years before that saith of Cyrus, " He is my shepherd and shall perform all my pleasure, even saying to Jerusalem, thou shalt be built ; and to the temple, thy foundation shall be laid."

When they commenced to build the second temple we are told by Ezra " that some of the Jews offered freely for the house of the Lord 61000 drams of gold, 5000 pounds of silver, and one hundred priests' garments, Ezra ii. 69 ; but still they never expected to build a temple in any way equal to Solomon's. There were five things wanting to make it as perfect as Solomon's: 1st, the tables of stone on which the law was written, which were in the ark when it was brought into his temple; 2nd the *Shekinah or divine presence in a cloud of glory on the mercy seat. 3rd, the Urim and Thummin, whence the oracle came, or divine answers to their inquiries ; 4th, the holy fire upon the altar, which came from heaven, and 5th, the spirit of prophecy, for though Haggai,

---

* The word Shekinah means, as used in Jewish history, that miraculous light or visible glory which was a symbol of the Divine presence ; it comes from *shaken*, to inhabit. The covering of the Ark was called the Mercy Seat, because God dwelt between the Cherubs in a body of light, Ex. xxv. 22. I will commune with thee from above the Mercy Seat, Lev. xvi. 2. For I will appear in the cloud upon the Mercy Seat. We heard the voice of one speak to him from off the Mercy Seat, Num. vii. 89.

Zachariah, and Malachi lived while the second temple was building, and prophecied after it was built, yet on their death, the prophetic spirit ceased from among them. After many hindrances, and twenty years of toil, the Jews again worshipped God in a temple in Jerusalem; and then Nehemiah the Jew built again the city of Jerusalem. St. Paul speaks of the tabernacle and sanctuary as things past, and tells us that the bodies of beasts for sacrifice were burnt without the camp, but the blood was brought into the sanctuary. Now, Jesus having shed his blood for the sins of the whole world, there seems no further need of a sanctuary; the Holy Spirit now reigns in every heart that is washed in Christ's blood. But as the sanctuaries were all attached to a temple, so every Christian must be a living member of the church or temple of God, if he wishes to make his heart a sanctuary for the Holy Spirit of God. Moses took the Tabernacle and put it without the camp, when he came from the Mount and found the people guilty of idolatry in making a golden calf. Exodus xxxiii. 7. But when the great Tabernacle was finished it stood within a large space of ground which was called the Court of the Tabernacle. Exodus xxvii. 9.

The word synagogue occurs but once in the Old Testament, that is in Psalm lxxiv, where it says, "They have burnt up all the synagogues in the land." But Christ tells us he taught in the synagogues, and in Acts xiii. we are told that Barnabas and others did the same. The word Church first occurs in Mat. xvi. 18, when Christ tells Peter "that upon this rock will I build my Church, and the gates of hell shall not prevail against it." Peter was of so impulsive a nature that he may at different times have sown the seeds of all the three Churches, which with their various branches are now spread all over the earth. He erred greatly when he asked to be allowed to build three churches, so great was the fault that it brought a voice from Heaven, but the voice did not say that he should not build three churches, but only tried to convince him that Christ was divine and therefore far superior to Moses and Elias. The Devil has divided Christians, but not destroyed Christianity. Christ, by his almighty power, foresaw the fierce warfare that the Devil would wage against it; how he would sow discord and even hatred among Christians; how some would lean on Peter, some on Paul and some on James, but the writer believes that the Greek, Roman and Protestant Churches (for all Protestant Churches that believe in the Trinity are one body, though some of them may have a diseased limb or joint out of place, causing them to be irritable and divided) will yet be re-united by the Holy Spirit of God, and then they will become one in faith and practise. Then tabernacles, temples, synagogues and churches will all send forth one united song of prayer and praise, and the hearts of the worshippers will be the sanctuary of our God.

Before concluding, let us look at the vestments about which there has been so much discussion lately. The common priests had a vest called an ephod and some peculiar garments of fine linen, which they used when they ministered in the tabernacle.—1 Sam. xxii. 18. But Aaron's garments, we are told in the Exodus xxxix., were of blue, purple and scarlet, besides the fine linen, verses 1, 27, 41. Indeed the High Priest's garments seem to consist of seven things, viz: the ephod, breast plate, girdle of curious work, robe of the ephod, the embroidered linen coat, and the mitre, with the golden plate.—Exod. xxviii. The ephod, which was worn by all the priests, was a sort of short vest without sleeves, made of fine linen with blue, purple and scarlet, interwoven with plates and wires of gold—Exodus xxxix. 2, 3, and worn over everything. The breast plate was made of the same work as the ephod, of a span square, with twelve jewels set in gold ranked in four rows of three each, and fastened to the ephod. As God used to make his will known to the High Priest by the Urim and Thummim in the breast plate, this cannot be necessary now, when God has sent his Son to be our High Priest, "For there is one God and one Mediator between God and man, the man Christ Jesus."— 1st Tim. ii. 5. But Christ left apostles, disciples and deacons to christianize the world; so that, though the High Priest's garments may be dispensed with, there is still need of a priestly garment, and as it is certain that no black garment was ever worn by a Jewish priest, does not the beautiful white robe seem the most appropriate, seeing that white is the emblem of purity, and that to be clothed in white is the privilege of those that overcome?—Rev. iii. "And to her was granted that she should be arrayed in fine linen, clean and white, for the fine linen is the righteousness of the Saints."—Rev. xix. 8. St. Paul tells us that Jesus is the High Priest over the house of God.— Heb. x. 21. In Mark xiv. 49, Christ says, "I was daily with you in the temple teaching." Christ's example is sufficient to prove the necessity of worshipping God in a temple made with hands, though in Acts vii. 47 it says that "Solomon built him an house; howbeit the Most High dwelleth not in temples made with hands," which certainly means that, though it is pleasing to God that he should be worshipped in a church or temple, still that it is in the sanctuary of the heart where he wishes to dwell, and the heart that loves his heavenly Father will seek him in his holy temple like a faithful, loving child.

"So shall his walk be close with God,
"Calm and serene his frame,
"So purer light shall mark the road
"That leads him to the Lamb."

And when the time is come that the earth shall be glorified, he will return and have his part in the first resurrection. To live on this earth for a thousand years without sickness, disease or death, is a privilege only to be enjoyed by those who are Christ's at his coming. Those who have resisted the temptations of the Devil through faith in Jesus; those who have been made perfect through suffering.—Ephesians iv. 13.

It does not appear in Scripture that the wicked receive any glorified body—they have no part in the first resurrection. This body will be the same as the one in which Christ appeared to his disciples after he rose from the dead, he was then so changed that Mary did not know him till he spoke to her, till he called her by name "Mary." Will he call us all by name? Then, when the disciples were assembled with closed doors, Christ appeared before them suddenly without opening the doors; this he never did before his death, and with this glorified body he ascended into Heaven: "while they beheld he was taken up."—Acts. i. 9.

The voice said he would come again, but when he comes, it will be as king, to reign over his kingdom, to reign supreme over the hearts of all the dwellers on the earth. When Christ came before, it was as a son under obedience. And at the end of all things he will appear as judge, when all who have ever lived on this earth, the wicked with their soil-stained garments, and the righteous in their glorified bodies, will receive their righteous sentence. The last enemy to be destroyed is death, so that death can have no power over these glorified bodies. Christ tells us in Mat. xxiii. 39, "Ye shall not see me henceforth till ye shall say, blessed is he that cometh in the name of the Lord." What a glorious time it will be to feel secured from the snares and temptations of the evil one, to feel free from this constant warfare, to feel that we are day by day becoming holier and better, more fitted to be angels in Heaven, learning day by day to know God, and to love him, and to feel that the time is approaching when we shall no longer see through a glass darkly, but face to face, striving constantly to make others happy instead of living for ourselves.

Money, the idol of the world, will then be shattered; there will be no such hoarding and gathering as there is now; each person will work so many hours a day, and all will have a living faith that God will provide, for he has said: "All the earth is mine."—Ex. xix. 5. "All the earth shall be filled with the glory of the Lord." Num. xiv. 21. "Take therefore no thought for the morrow; for the morrow shall take thought for the things of itself."—Mat. vi. 34. May all Christians look at the signs of the times; all things are teaching us that a change is coming; we know not how soon we may hear the voice saying: "Praise our God, all ye his servants, and ye that fear Him, both small and great; and I heard as it were the voice of great multitudes, and as the voice of many waters, and as the voice of mighty thunderings, saying, Alleluia: for the Lord God omnipotent reigneth."—Rev. xx. 5-6. "Even so, come, Lord Jesus. The Grace of our Lord Jesus Christ be with you all. Amen." Rev. xxii. 2.

Considering the following worthy of notice, I insert it here:—

In reading a book the other day, I was struck with the following remarks:—"As God was both the Jewish God and King, the Tabernacle and the Temple may be considered not only as the residence of their God, but also as the palace of their King; also the Court of the Tabernacle was the Court of the Palace; the Holy of Holies was the Presence Chamber, the Mercy Seat was his throne. The Cherubs represented his attendants as God, and the Priests were his Ministers of State as King; the Levites his Officers dispersed through his Kingdom. The table of Show Bread, together with the sacrifices which were given to the Priest, represented the provision for his household."

And Josephus says, that the two parts of the Tabernacle which were accessible to the Priests, denoted the Land and the Sea. But the third part, which was for God alone, represented Heaven, which is inaccessible to men. The twelve loaves on the Table stood for our twelve months; the seven lamps, the seven planets; the four vials, the four elements; the plain linen, the earth, because flax grows in the earth. The purple signified the sea, because that colour is dyed by the blood of a sea shell fish; the blue, the air; the scarlet, fire; the ephod shewed that God had made the universe of four elements, and the gold related to the splendour by which all are enlightened. Breast plate in the middle of the ephod resembled the earth, for that has the middle place in the world. The two buttons on the priests' shoulder, stood for the sun and moon.

Through this year that's just begun
Let us every Idol shun.
The Holy Spirit comes to reign,
To wipe away all tears and pain.

May women in one bond unite
To crush the wrong and do the right.
Then men and angels soon will sing
Praise to God our Heavenly King.

When love in every household dwells
Then gaily ring the marriage bells;
The sword will in its scabbard rust,
And all will in the Saviour trust.

The tree of life we then shall taste
No more our energies shall waste;
Our goodness, truth and love alone
Will fit us then to fill a Throne.

ADAM'S SIN.

'Tis sad to think of all the crime
   One act of selfish pleasure cost,
Spread vice around in every clime,
   All man's spir'tual eyesight lost.

No longer innocent and pure,—
   They thought themselves from God to hide,
With lame excuses tried to cure
   The sin for which their God did chide.

Soon envy fill'd the human mind,
   And caus'd a brother's blood to flow,
For angry passions Cain did blind,
   And Abel died beneath his blow.

When Adam, Eve, and Cain first look'd
   On sin's first fruits, sweet Abel's death,
Their limbs with horror must have shook,
   They lost their sight and he his breath.

Hope still remains, with faith to guide,
   Goodness may yet man's breath retain,
For God will not his children chide,
   When from their sins they do abstain.

Christ liv'd and died that men may learn
   Never to taste forbidden fruit;
Mankind might surely now discern
   Evil will not their Maker suit.

Satan has for many a day
   With his passions hearts defil'd,
Faith, hope, and love has hid away,
   And with his doubts and fears beguil'd.

His anger first shed human blood,
    And taught men to deceive and lie;
Man's works drove God to send a flood,
    When almost all the race did die.

When man puts from him all his fear,
    And in his God does firmly trust,
He will his footsteps once more hear,
    And feel that God is good and just.

For Christ has shed his blood in love,
    In order that mankind may live,
May welcome back the heavenly Dove,
    And with the angels glory give.

Soon may this end accomplish'd be,
    The electric tie draws mind to mind,
Soon may our spirits learn to see,
    And know that God is ever kind.

The Devil's sway will then be past,
    This kingdom then our Lord's become,
God's reign will then for ever last,
    His will on earth be ever done.

Come sisters, virgins, arm and try
If death's last arrows we can fly;
If from the earth the curse we rake,
Death will this kingdom then forsake.

When we our passions all subdue,
And give to God what is his due,
Like Jesus try with all our might
To walk as always in his sight,

His guidance follow day by day,
In sleep our souls on Jesus lay;
His blood will wash out all the stains,
And draw us with his gentle reins.

Our homes will be a scene of bliss,
The virtues will each other kiss;
Labour and love together wed,
New light will on our path be shed.

Our bodies will not waste away,
But stronger grow from day to day;
Like lions, overcome the foe,
And God will banish all our woe.

Like eagles soar with God on high,
And we will see beyond the sky;
What glories we shall then behold!
Jesus will all to us unfold.

Like oxen, work and labor hard,
To plough the heart and plant the word,
Seed of union we will sow,
And all in grace together grow.

The Shepherd then his lambs will call,
Jews and Turks and Christians all,
One Ark will build and enter in,
And all will then have done with sin.

And to the earth then will return
Saints, prophets, fathers, all to learn
That Christ the victory has claim'd,
And death and hell will both be chain'd.

The thousand years will on us dawn,
Earth's idols we will learn to scorn;
With chain and key the dragon bound,
All peaceful we will walk around.

AN ALLEGORY.

A ship sets gaily out to sea,
   With all her colors flying,
The crew as busy as a bee,
   All storms and gales defying.

At first her course is very smooth,
   The sailors whistle and sing,
The pilot leaves with lines to soothe,
   Those whose hearts a parting wring.

How confidently each one talks
   Of the land they hope to reach,
And as upon the deck they walk,
   Think of homes they will besiege.

When lo! a grating sound is heard,
   Now fear shakes each human frame,
Some rocks! some rocks! are whispered,—
   All the life boat try to gain.

One voice alone is calm and strong,
   He says, wait and make ready,
She has not struck, so come along
   And try to keep her steady.

They work and strive, but all in vain,
   The rudder soon gets broken,
Water dashes through each pane—
   Not many words are spoken.

The ship seems doom'd, they fear they soon
   Will sink beneath the ocean;
The night was dark, no cheerful moon—
   The wind kept her in motion.

Four anchors from the stern was cast,
    And for the day they pray'd;
Some thought it best to make her fast,
    So in the ship they stay'd.

The sun peep'd out, light always cheering,
    Fresh strength to their courage gave;
Slowly now the ship they're steering,
    Through shoals, and rocks, and caves.

Sailors and crew united toil,
    To pass the dangerous cliffs,
The anchors rise, the ropes they coil,
    She floats and then she shifts.

The danger past, how thankful all
    To the one who never yielded,
When for the life boat all did call,
    His prayers their errors shielded.

The Church now shakes from stem to stern
    With great and small divisions,
Christians unite and Christ-like learn,
    God's love has no partitions.

FOR THE PLYMOUTH BRETHREN.

Christ's words are, "blessed are the meek,
    For they shall inherit the earth,"
Thus the patient yet may seek
    A great reign of glorious mirth.

Methinks I hear "come blessed, come,"
    The kingdom is prepar'd for you;
From the beginning Christ my Son
    Has promis'd life for all those who,

With faith and patience, hope and joy,
  Strive all their God's commands to keep,
Who find the gold without alloy,
  Which in his book is hidden deep.

These at his table drink and eat,
  Many shall come from east and west,
With all the prophets take their seat,
  And God will give them of the best.

In them the twelve tribes judges see,
  All on thrones they shall be seated,
This kingdom then our Lord's will be,
  Satan's schemes be all defeated.

On David's throne then Christ will reign,
  And round him all his sheep will sing;
Wash'd in his blood from every stain,
  The air will loud with praises ring.

This second Eden men behold,
  Look forward but a little space,
For those glories and joys untold,
  Which all who conquer them will taste.

O hasten the day of his coming,
  Our swords into ploughshares beating,
Spears into pruning hooks turning,
  Isaac and Jacob awaking.

Then the earth will its garments change,
  Righteousness it will put on;
The Devil will not then derange
  The stones in the temple of God.

For the spirit with love's cement,
  Will each stone to its place restore,
With holiness and truth prevent
  Sin over ent'ring at the door.

When the great corner stone returns,
    Each jewel will find its place,
He who o'ercomes and evil spurns,
    Will see his dear Saviour's face.

SIN OF SWEARING.

WRITTEN BY REQUEST OF J. C. L.

Children to school for knowledge go,
    The world its ways to learn,
That they, when they do older grow,
    Their bread themselves may earn.

Some go to it quite willingly,
    Acquiring, day by day
Some new ideas, pleasantly
    To cheer them on their way.

Some with a sad, reluctant air,
    Without a steady aim,
Find everywhere some little snare,
    Their thoughts and time to claim.

Like pretty summer butterflies,
    They taste each little sweet;
Never labouring for a prize,
    Their minds they daily cheat.

Then evil words fill up the space,
    They learn to curse and swear:
The Christian name they thus disgrace,
    And for Satan's rule prepare.

Masters then in Passions fly,
    When bad boys them provoke,
These boys then quickly tell a lie,
    And walk in Satan's yoke.

As good and evil seed we find,
  Our pathway doth surround;
Certain plain rules should surely bind,
  Or weeds will fill the ground.

Bad words like stinging wasps to flee,
  Let school boys be agreed,
And each, like an industrious bee,
  His soul and body feed.

Then all will very careful be,
  What from the mouth proceeds;
Begin each day with bended knee,
  To plant some Holy Seeds.

The food that in the mouth we place,
  We cleanse and purify;
But oaths which will destroy our race,
  Come forth without a sigh.

Your words like purest honey, should
  Make all your pathway smooth;
That like a tree which years has stood,
  A standard you will prove.

The bees a solemn lesson teach,
  Which young minds should apply;
Each little bee to us does preach,
  And food for us supply.

Not only for their daily wants,
  Do the bees provide some food;
But men in earth's most dreary haunts,
  Have found their honey good.

The Baptist on it did subsist,
  With locusts for his meat,
When gaining strength to pierce the mist
  Of earth's great winding sheet.

Then masters, schoolboys, one and all,
   At once try some new plan,
That all may as before the fall,
   See Christ again as man.

Each day, in three you should divide.
   Be just in all you do;
Let not the morning from you slide
   Till God has had his due.

The body then demands your care,
   Its wants are not a few,
Give it, oh, give it but its share,
   Or you will have to rue.

Books and works of various kinds,
   The third part will engross;
E'en through these pathways Satan winds,
   Of great minds he can boast.

Then watch and trim your lamps anew,
   Lay in a store of oil,
For soon God's own beloved Jew
   Will share with us the spoil.

Darkness and light still represent,
   The spirit that will guide;
Now chosen by our own consent,
   Hereafter to preside.

Our will is free to make the choice,
   Now we ourselves enlist,
God speaks to us in tender voice,
   The tempter to resist.

When he beguiles with trifling arts,
   And glittering golden toys;
Purloining, snaring, binding hearts,
   Concealing God's pure joys.

A WONDERFUL LIGHT SEEN IN THREE RIVERS JULY, 1873.

What strange light is this I see,
    Shedding such a lustre round;
Can it a faint shadow be,
    That thy truth will soon abound?

That the things which chain and bind
    All thy creatures here on earth,
Pierc'd by rays of some new kind,
    Will produce some lasting mirth?

It lights the country far and wide,
    Encircles each shrub and tree;
The boats and vessels as they glide,
    Newly painted seem to be.

Lake St. Peter glitters so,
    That we gaze with rapture great;
To my mind it seems to show
    Earth's glorious future state.

When our tabernacles three,
    Which St. Peter did design,
Will united plant the tree,
    And the ever-living vine,

Of which, when our souls partake,
    Pure and holy hearts we gain;
Satan foil'd, will us forsake,
    When Christ in our hearts does reign.

None will labor then in vain,
    Those that plant good fruit will eat,
And all youthful will remain,
    Till Messiah they do greet.

When he comes some to reward,
   Seated on his Mighty throne,
Many now who call Christ, Lord,
   I fear he will then disown.

The Glory he with him will bring,
   Will brighten all below;
Saints and angels then will fling
   A vail over sin and woe.

And what prophets have foretold,
   Which is hard to comprehend,
They will to us all unfold,
   And our doubts and fears will end.

May the Jews at once begin
   To regenerate the earth,
So that Satan, death and sin
   Shall no longer mar our mirth.

Then the Father, Spirit, Son,
   So much glory will reveal,
That the light of moon and sun
   It will from us quite conceal.

Darkness then all disappears
   Before this great wondrous light,
Christ will dry up all our tears,
   And restore our long-lost sight.

Then with one united chime,
   Alleluia we will sing,
And through all and ev'ry clime,
   Shall its echoes joyful ring.

Past, Present, and Future.

Past, Present and Future must be my Theme,
That some of their errors we may redeem.
Past, which is gone, never more to return,
Present, in which men and women may learn
That none are unselfish enough on earth
To love you, because of your virtuous worth;
So, in future our thoughts must soar above
To Him, who lives in the region of love;
And pray Him to send down heavenly peace,
To cause all discords and passions to cease;
To make goodness triumph, and never yield
Till the tempter is driven from the field;
His gold may glitter, his pleasures may please,
His surrounding wealth may give men some ease,
But they know not the moment death may call,
And scatter their idols and treasures, all.
But the faith to use our wealth, while in health,
To glorify God, regardless of self,
Will sift Satan's schemes, his stubble will burn,
To his own dark region he will return,
Fleeing from earth in rage and despair
At the sight of Christ in His regal chair,—
For, when his spiritual reigns begins,
The Christian his crown of glory wins—
The trials and sorrows of earth will end—
Deceivers and liars to hell descend.

THE PAST.

Once, pure love from heaven
God center'd in Eden,—
Eve's face then did shine
With God's glory divine,—
All was wholesome and good;
On the trees grew their food.
Beasts and birds, great and small,
Then attended man's call;
Sin on earth, then unknown,
Was in Paradise sown.

PRESENT.

Now, if selfish and vain,
You can the men entertain;
You may just lie and deceive;
And, like a regular Eve,
Flirt with one and another,
Give them plenty of bother,
They will run with their money
And call you, my honey!

FUTURE.

Fed with holy food,
Strengthened from above;
Daily doing good.
Labouring with love,
Singing songs of praise,
With a cheerful will,
Working day by day,
Shunning all that's ill,
Living like the just,
Generous and kind,
All around us must
Daily blessings find.

Never deceiving,
A foe or a friend,
Ever believing
Christ soon will descend.

7th LUKE.

Into a city called Nain
   Christ with much people went,
At the gate he beheld, with pain,
   A widow whose heart was rent

With anguish sore: her only son
   Was stretch'd upon his bier,
All joy for her on earth was done,—
   When Jesus himself drew near.

Weep not, Christ to the widow said,
   Young man do thou now arise,
The dead sat up and spake, Christ led
   Him to her before all eyes.

Lazarus, Jairus and this youth
   Christ rais'd from death to life,
He taught us how to walk in truth,
   And conquer in the strife.

Christ said a little while must pass
   Before he claim'd his Bride,
That time is passing, but alas!
   The Bride does her beauty hide.

Beneath a weight of pomp and show
   Her sweet graces three are lost,
She must be humbled and brought low,
   No mattor how great the cost.

When she has purified her faith,
   Stript all her vain idols bare,
She will the great voice hear that saith
   My tabernacle is there.

21st JOHN, 23.

I will that thou shalt tarry
    In space until I come,
Hasten, Lord, thy church to marry,
    And all to fold in one.

Then all the saints and martyrs,
    Who tarry, Lord, for thee;
The voice of many waters,
    To thee will bend the knee.

Christ comes not to a manger,
    With friends a very few,
Nor as a weary stranger,
    To ask what is his due:

On a White Horse him behold,
    He the Faithful and true,
Many crowns of shining gold,
    A name that no man knew.

A vesture dipped in blood,
    Our God will bring to light,
With his armies like a flood,
    In linen pure and white.

THE SHIELD OF FAITH.

This world is a great battle field,
    Where Evil has triumphed long;
Faith is now the Christian shield,
    And Hope is his constant song.

The Faith that our Maker requires
    Is a real and a living thing;
It is yielding the heart's desire,
    If it leads to any sin.

'Tis the feeling that God knows best,
   That his hand directs the way;
It is laying our hearts to rest,
   And doing his will each day.

Our Saviour, gentle and kind,
   Taught us God's will must be done,
But we are so dreadfully blind,
   His work we try to shun.

As soon as living Faith prevails,
   The Battle draws to an end;
The Devil never men assails,
   When their armour does defend.

Through our Idols he now assaults
   And then he our hearts surrounds,
Then pursuing he never halts,
   Till he pierces and confounds.

O cast then our dead Faith away,
   Of time give God the tenth;
Let Christ's example be our stay,
   God's Spirit will give us strength.

PATIENCE.

Like Jonah we do fast and pray,
In God's own appointed way,
But oh how sadly we contend,
With the trials that he sends.

Our Father must know what is best,
He is right our Faith to test;
If we could all our wishes gain,
What confusion would prevail.

Then let us be content and wise,
Daily blessings learn to prize,
Submissive when he takes away,
Looking for a brighter day.

The love that God to us has shown,
Ought to melt our hearts of stone,
Should teach us all events to trust
To the only Wise and Just.

If for God's laws we show much zeal
Bitter words men make us feel.
The world does not such understand,
They are mocked on ev'ry hand.

Daily we must patient grow,
Though the waves of trouble flow;
Endurance is a virtue great,
Loving we must watch and wait.

God will in time accept the meek,
They are those Christ came to seek;
Every trial God does send,
Is intended to amend,

To purify and make us clean,
Raise our thoughts to things unseen;
Prepare us for that glorious time,
When life will become divine.

MATTHEW vi. 24.

Two masters now men try to please,
  This Christ said he could not do,
And yet man uses every nerve
  His body's cravings to pursue.

Each one has some besetting sin,
    Which he needs to hold in check,
Or Satan will contrive to spin
    A web that poor soul to wreck.

No ray of light can penetrate,
    When the web he does complete;
His angels guard so well the gate,
    That it forms his winding sheet.

The heart that did unwind his skein,
    Unravel all Satan's scheme,
Does well deserve Messiah's name,
    For his work our souls redeem.

His daily life so perfect, pure,
    Though temptations did assail;
The lame, the blind and deaf did cure,
    Yes, and over death prevail.

Hark! the solemn funeral bell,
    Of Christ the Saviour dear,
He died to rescue man from hell,
    To make him both see and hear

The mighty God who Adam knew,
    When on earth he first was plac'd;
And pardon for the sins to sue,
    Of this race by sin disgrac'd.

But man for whom this work was done,
    Still pursues his evil ways,
He will not selfish pleasures shun—
    Like Felix, waits future days.

The heavens shook, the earth did quake,
    When Christ hung up on the cross,
The darkness made men's bodies shake
    Yea, their souls were tempest-tost.

He travell'd to the spirit's land,
    And there set the captives free,
His followers, a little band,
    Did his resurrection see.

They saw his body that was pierc'd,
    With great agony and pain,
But oh! how soon their sorrow ceas'd,
    When they heard his voice again.

Before them all he did ascend
    To his mansion in the skies,
His spirit will on all descend,
    When his love alone we prize.

This world would be the land of life,
    Perpetual youth would reign,
If all would try, and work, and strive,
    To earn a christian name.

The flaming sword that guards the gate
    Would guide us and give us light;
The Seraphim that always wait,
    Would restore the Tree of Life.

Nations all awake, arise,
    Be virtuous in your youth;
As soon as men are really wise,
    They'll aim for eternal truth.

The curse will not then mar the scene,
    Christ his ensign will display,
And his five sacraments will gleam,
    With a bright electric ray,

Which will in time restore the sight,
    That has from our spirits fled,
And will forever put to flight
    All the misery and dread

Which Adam brought upon the race,
    When he tasted Satan's sweets,
Which still all eagerly embrace,
    When he cunningly entreats.

He thus controls men's hearts on earth,
    In his old deceitful way,
Giving a little short-liv'd mirth,
    For their homage day by day.

But when our hearts we all prepare
    For Christ's spiritual reign,
Satan will not our souls ensnare,
    Nor will death our bodies claim.

As Messiah Christ then will come,
    His victory to maintain,
And with the splendor of the sun,
    Will appear the righteous slain.

THE CONSCIENCE.

O how we long the voice to hear,
Of the one our soul holds dear;
Do we thus welcome that still voice,
Saying, good must be your choice.

Every creature feels its power
Speaking in Temptation's hour,
Beware, desist, it is a sin,
Keep all pure and bright within.

In every age and every zone
All have heard its gentle tone,
Thus none can say they never knew
God with man does ever sue.

Some say, God does predestinate
And destruction is their fate;
God has forechosen his elect,
They may well be circumspect.

But with a will as free as air,
Conscience whispering beware,
Thoughts such as these must be untrue,
This our God could never do.

Man daily does Christ crucify
When God's spirit they defy;
Let altogether hear and heed,
And such thorns and thistles weed.

Then to God's will we all will bow,
And to keep his law will vow,
Images, idols, all must fall,
For his still small voice does call.

THE SABBATH DAY.

The Sabbath day, the Sabbath day,
 A precious gift to man;
O that I could in this my lay,
 All its glories fairly scan.

Six days of strife and contest great
 Again have passed away,
O may we ere, it is too late,
 Feel precious that great day.

'Twas by a Heavenly Father made,
 For knowledge of him to gain,
Six days the earth in order laid,
 The seventh his power sustain.

Our earthly parents ask that we
    Should learn to love and fear them;
We must very plainly see
    When God speaks we must hear him.

Six thousand years are nearly past
    Since one day's rest he ordered,
Man will I fear until the last,
    Be selfish, proud, disorder'd.

But when these past, the time of rest,
    Which quickly is approaching,
Bursts forth with joy and with a zest,
    For those whose lamps are burning.

How will those feel who all their share
    Of time and rest have wasted;
They cannot think that we will spare
    Our oil, when we have tasted—

The pleasures and the happiness
    God for us has provided;
Oh no! we then will love them less,
    And care not where they're hided.

But oh! once more I pray that all
    Will listen to their Maker,
At once, before the angels call,
    Be one with their Creator.

For when he comes as King to reign,
    With glory o'er his Kingdom;
This world he frees from ev'ry pain,
    Drives Death from this Dominion.

THE MILLENNIUM.

The reign of Christ draws near,
Soon, soon he will appear,
He then will claim his Bride,
And for her wants provide.

The bridal robes prepare,
With pure bright jewels rare,
Fine linen clean and white,
Bring forth for her to light.

Your voices tune to sing
Alleluia to the King,
With the saints and martyrs,
Voice of many waters,

And mighty thunderings,
Then suddenly there springs
One startling song of praise,
Which earth to Heav'n will raise.

And being glorified
With love electrified,
Then spiritual light
Will shine for ever bright.

And under his own vine,
In that bright happy time,
Will each man with his wife,
Enjoy the things of life.

STRAY LEAVES.

STRAY LEAVES.

To the memory of the Rev. Dean Bethune, who was Rector of Montreal Cathedral for nearly half a century.

Worms of the earth, why so much pride?
In the grave yard side by side,
See kings and nobles and our dean,
With the poor, the vile, the mean.

This worthy priest has passed away,
And his body turned to clay,
His spirit soars in space alone,
In that place on earth unknown.

He is now waiting at the shore,
Christ, who is himself the door,
Drawing him to his blessed fold,
Saints and martyrs to behold.

He held for nearly three score years,
In this vale of woe and tears,
Office of deacon, priest and dean,
Always cheerful, calm, serene.

And when with Jesus he returns,
With the crown the christian earns,
Evil will not his course impede,
Nor his heart be made to bleed.

Archdeacons, rectors, canons, deans,
Great high-sounding names it seems,
But I have searched but never found,
In the Bible any ground

For any of these mighty four,
Which are increasing by the score;
Bishops, priests, and deacons though,
Were to combat with the foe.

These our christian orders three,
Are as plain as plain can be,
The others great confusion make,
To their folly pray awake.

If for peace you all really sigh,
Let these foolish trifles die;
Strive to be honest, just and true,
You will reap the honor due.

LINES WRITTEN ON THE CHURCH IN THREE RIVERS WHICH AFTER BEING USED AS A MONASTERY, AND COURT HOUSE BECAME AN EPISCOPAL CHURCH AND HAS LATELY BEEN MODERNIZED.

The oldest church in this our land
Surrounded by Three Rivers stands;
Many histories it can tell,
For it has wrung their dying knell.

First jolly monks its niches fill'd,
And round it many acres till'd,
They, like their fathers, idols had,
Or still with bodies would be clad.

Their deeds of goodness or of sin
Have left no mark or trace within,
None these will know until the time
That Jesus' reign begins to shine.

A time of war brought changes round,
And judges on its benches found
That they within those walls should hold
Judgment on sinners from the fold.

These also had their time and day,
And like the monks have passed away;
But some of them will soon return,
And with their fellows live and learn.

That had they lived as Jesus did,
They in the earth would not be hid.
Then all our idols we will burn,
And a Christian name will earn.

Again it saw another change,
The law the priests again derange,
And rob'd and mitred weekly sung,
Their voices high in praises rung.

When it was curious and quaint,
Some persons thought it needed paint,
Forgetting what our Saviour taught,
They old and new together wrought.

First they put God's commands aside,
Which should all congregations guide,
Every altar they should grace,
This seems to be their proper place.

The Dove, the emblem of God's love,
Hovering o'er them from above,
Imparts to them no mystic sign,
They must replace with new design.

And gaudy figures now are seen
Where this symbol once did gleam,
Are figures in their proper place,
When they do the Altar grace?

The Dove each temple should adorn,
Without it we must ever mourn.
The one that from the Ark did soar,
May we soon to our Ark restore.

O Earth, earth, earth at once attend,
Begin and all your ways amend;
Jesus, David's righteous branch,
A perfect temple soon will launch.

The Spirit urges me to write,
To bid you walk as in his sight,
That when his work is well begun
You may not find yourselves undone.

Make one great purifying change,
Which will our errors all arrange,
Unite us all in Christ's great cause,
And teach us all to keep his laws.

Not one or two for fear of man,
Which before God is but a sham,
But sifting ev'ry thought and word,
Knowing God all has seen and heard.

Then the holy heavenly Dove
Will bind us with the cords of love,
Making us one in thought and deed,
One Baptism, and one holy creed.

THE FALLS OF NIAGARA.

Niagara, thou wonder!
  With ever ceaseless roar,
Thy immeasurable water,
  Whose great unfailing store

For centuries has steadily
   Been pouring o'er these rocks,
Some escaping stealthily,
   The mighty vortex mocks.

All quickly disappearing
   Beneath a placid brow,
To the whirlpool receding,
   Can any tell us how?

None but the Great Creator,
   To whom our thoughts must rise,
The one originator
   Of earth, sea, air and skies.

This vast flowing cataract,
   God in his wisdom made,
The builder, the architect,
   Here has well portray'd.

That eternal bliss or woe,
   For man so long design'd,
Whither all do daily row
   Each to his place assign'd.

See that lovely shade of green,
   Beneath the rapid foam;
Giving man a little gleam
   Of a bright future home.

Then in that beauteous spray,
   We may easily discern
The bright glorified array,
   That God's chosen ones will earn.

When, as in the burning springs,
   Fire from the waters blaze,
Christ with healing in his wings,
   With love will all amaze.

    And beneath a bridal veil,
      Our differences cease;
    The Messiah all will hail,
      God's Spirit give us peace.

THE GREAT BOAT RACE ON THE KENEBECASIS.

A boat race, 'tis a sight to see,
The St. John's against England free,
The men well trained for action,
With certain food and good tuition.

Their minds on it for months were bent,
Ev'ry energy on it spent,
Constant thought by night and by day,
To gain a victory they say.

Great crowds assemble on the wharf,
How eager all to see them off;
They start, and England shouts ahead,
When their champion drops his head.

The race of life for him is done,
And what has all his hard work won,
Another man jumps in the boat,
And soon they are again afloat.

A little shock men have receiv'd,
Still evil will them all deceive,
It never strikes them something's wrong
With all that vast and motley throng.

Death no more arrows here would shoot
If man would hear his Maker's suit,
Keep all his passions in control,
And train and gently feed the soul.

A boat race it should be a sight
In which all men might take delight,
Were it once stript of all the vice
Which now men think so very nice.

The idol now that makes men sin
Is bright without and black within;
It gives them pleasure for a day,
And guides them on their downward way

For Renforth this time's life is o'er,
Four doctors cannot him restore,
Nor priestly lore nor human skill,
Can change the great Creator's will.

God speaks, he sends this cross to move
Mankind to worship him in love,
In active sports men may delight
If they but keep their God in sight.

THE BOSTON JUBILEE OF 1872.

Great country, England's daughter
   Hail thy time of jubilee,
Gather'd from ev'ry quarter,
   All nations sing with thee.

Joy and peace you well combine,
   Discords thus will pass away,
Love to man in this does shine,
   You have reason to be gay.

Open'd well with praise to God,
   Psalm of old, sweet voices sing,
Instruments, with one accord,
   Make the very timbers ring.

One angelic voice is heard,
   Whose sweet notes all hearts entrance,
This fine German singing bird,
   Gives to higher joys a glance.

English, Prussian, German, French,
   Four great bands with yours unite,
Sounds and din of war thus quench,
   Is a grand and beauteous sight.

Pilgrim fathers would rejoice
   If they heard these peaceful strains,
Thousands singing with one voice,
   Proves that Satan's kingdom wanes.

ON KING'S CHAPEL, THE OLDEST CHURCH
IN BOSTON, BUILT FOR AN EPISCOPALIAN CHURCH NOW USED AS A UNITARIAN.

A fine old church in Boston stands,
   Built the three in One to Praise.
The form they still hold in their hands,
   It now wrong belief conveys.

The Evil one has made this change,
   Taught men to doubt God's power;
He tries his worship to derange,
   And makes himself their tower.

Men who in God's own image made,
   Body, mind and soul possess,
Ought to tremble and be afraid,
   Their Creator to address.

Without the aid of God the Son
   And the Spirit for their guest;
The great I am, the Three in One,
   Bids us build in Christ our nest.

To those who feel he is Divine
  A Rock that no storm can shake;
But sand that flies before the wind,
  If we from him this power take.

O that my verse could penetrate,
  Could pierce like a two-edged sword,
The worshippers who sit in state
  Where Satan is thus ador'd.

LINES

WRITTEN ON HEARING OF THE GREAT FIRE IN CHICAGO IN 1871.

This planet bright and blooming made,
With sin is covered with a shade;
Evil has made for it a pall
Which hangs about it since the Fall.

This blight which causes life to cease,
Which all our hopes from us does fleece,
Is draping all the earth in cloud
For Fire and Sword are flying round.

The Evil Spirit war has waged,
And like a Lion he has raged
To see his glory on the wane,
His idols broken like a pane.

In ten years time a city sprung,
The theme of all and every tongue;
Money was there so quickly coined
That some were thought to have purloined.

So prosperous they had become
That evil they forgot to shun;
Their joy has all been turned to woe,
New seed they must begin to sow.

Men toil and strive with pain and tears
To gather gold for future years,
And in an hour this precious hoard
Is swept away from off the board.

For Fire—that direful, dreadful, scourge,
Has rais'd a loud and dismal dirge;
Their gourds have all been swept away,
And prov'd themselves but worthless clay.

Oh! that I could men's spirits raise,
Prepare them for those brighter days,
That mighty reign of Christ on earth
When all will have a second birth.

ON THE WISCONSIN FIRES IN 1871.

A fire, behold it blazes bright,
It is a grand imposing sight,
To see tall and towering trees
Lighting skies and neighboring seas.

Serpent-like it coils round and round,
And trails itself along the ground,
Destroying all within its reach,
The course of sin it does us teach.

Scores of men in a barn did hide,
But on and on the fire did glide,
Their groans and moans it heeded not,
Nothing but ashes marks the plot.

All things now have a mournful air,
Hearts seem all so opprest with care,
These trials are uniting lands,
For see them with extended hands.

England like a good old mother
Sends gold guineas to her daughter;
Canada, a loving sister,
Sends her salve to heal the blister.

The other states their lavish wealth
Send to restore their sister's health,
This is the way to sheath the swords,
To scatter round our heaps and hoards.

Such great love is a sight to see,
Distrust and envy soon will flee,
Christian work begins to dawn,
Soon we will hear the angel's horn.

What a glorious sound to those
Who on Messiah's love repose,
Twelve gates of pearl will them enclose,
The Tree of Life God will disclose.

ON THE OCCASION OF NINE PEOPLE BEING POISONED, FROM DRINKING STOLEN WINE, AND DYING IN HERMINE STREET, MONTREAL.

Sad and tragic are the scenes
  We daily see and hear;
Very short-liv'd are the dreams
  Of bliss in sin's career.

See those poor benighted souls,
  Who drank that stolen wine,
Which within like burning coals
  Of poison soon gave sign.

What is the end of their joy,
  Their nights of noisy mirth,
Their own idol did destroy
  Yes, swept them from the earth.

For at this, their last carouse,
　Their greedy appetite
The Lord's angel did arouse,
　Quite suddenly to smite.

Both young and old with horror
　Felt poison in their veins,
And then upon the morrow
　Death seven of them claims.

Some days pass and other two
　Were cold and lifeless clay,
Others all their life will rue
　Sin's poisonous decay.

The Tempter with drink did lead
　Them to both lie and steal,
O, that with me all agreed
　On sin to plant their heel.

By setting his snares aside,
　Examining their worth,
Then God's spirit will us guide,
　Regenerating the earth.

Producing much purer wheat,
　Unsullied by a tare,
Satan then will cease to reap,
　For we will all beware.

Then, fastening on the shield
　Of faith and love entwin'd,
Sin's fiery darts must yield,
　For God's truth will us bind.

And with unity and peace,
　God's praises will resound,
And our bodies then will cease
　To moulder in the ground

AN ADDRESS TO THE FREEMASONS.

Freemasons, I implore your aid
Satan's kingdom to invade;
God will restore the tree of life
When we sheath the sword of strife.

For near six thousand years, with pride
Sin has turn'd mankind aside,
With malicious cunning art,
From the great Creator's chart.

A glorious army let us make
To defeat this wily snake;
Then we shall find the narrow way
Leading to eternal day.

Once plant the seed I wish to sow,
Man will bid adieu to woe,
And Adam's sons will then regain
What was lost by sin and shame.

When Eve and Adam sins did chase
Them from Eden in disgrace;
Your craft for truth have always wrought,
I for years, for it have sought.

It is the thing that we must find,
It must flourish in each mind;
Instead of sparkling now and then,
It must be the one great gem

Lighting the features of each face,
With a new and beaut'ous grace;
The eyes must brighten with its beams,
And send forth its holy gleams.

This is the sacred, mystic tie
For which now we all do sigh:
Not Masonic Fraternity,
But pure Christianity.

A Brotherhood we then shall see,
With a thirty-fourth degree;
Joining its members link to link,
Ere their shatter'd ark does sink.

These will worship the great *I Am*,
And work out his wondrous plan,
Not as our many creeds require;
But with one great blaze of fire.

Extracting truth from each and all,
They will to their minds recall
The promises to Abram made,
When he such strong faith displayed,—

As to offer his dearest son,
Type of God's own precious one;
Who left the great Jehovah's throne,
That for sin he might atone,

This mighty, wondrous sacrifice
Some completely mystifies,
They cannot, will not comprehend
That their God did condescend

The evil spirit's scheme to foil,
From his grasp to snatch the spoil;
My work has with the Spirit's aid,
Satan's scheming well portray'd.

Written in plain and simple form,
Of all classic learning shorn,
It aims to influence the heart,
Tracing for it virtue's chart.

When it is altogether bound,
Its truth will the Jews astound;
God's work in it they will perceive,
And on Christ they will believe.

The Builder of the Universe
Then will ease us of the curse;
Our grand and grac'ous architect
Will sin from the earth eject.

Around the cross we then shall see
Christians, Jews and Turks all three;
The heathen seeing such unite,
Will enquire about the light.

To Jesus they will bend the knee,
His love then from sin will free;
By encircling this church, the vine,
We advance this happy time.

In Christ, we trace the rock or stone
Which in the first temple shown,
The latter house will this reveal,
When with truth and words we seal.

The oldest symbol that science knows,
The triangle will disclose;
The five mysterious means of grace,
God has offer'd to the race,

And which in fellowship will bind
God with all the human kind;
When they of them in faith partake,
And their sins do all forsake.

Though but a small, five-pointed star,
It may end the Christian war;
Then perfect health we shall enjoy,
The *Pentalpha well employ.

---

* The Triple Temple is called in Masonry The Pentalpha and is the Symbol of Health.

The broken square will then unite,
Darkness will give place to light,
Beauty and wisdom from above,
Will combine with strength and love.

To make man perfect and upright,
One in whom God can delight,
He will not then, as now decay,
Nor to Satan homage pay.

The three in one, the great *I Am*,
Will restore to earth and man
The calm and peaceful, holy days,
On which Adam once did gaze.

A leaf from Palestine, quite green,
In your hands last year was seen;
The Brotherhood this did elate,
For from thence they emanate.

My leaves more pleasure will convey,
They more lasting joys display;
And when their precepts fill each soul,
Christ will come and make us whole.

For his Spirit my hand does guide,
And his work it is to chide;
Of sin, he said he would convince
Both the peasant and the prince.

It was an Eve, the poison gave,
That made Adam Satan's slave;
Another Eve now bids you wake,
And his chains forever break.

A CHILD'S POEM.

A little maid with golden hair
   Said, read me now another,
A poem such as you have there,
   For me and for my brother.

Now just like two pretty flowers,
   That once in a garden grew,
You gather from gentle showers,
   A sunnier brighter hue.

That is, if in your daily course
   You your various duties do,
By drawing from a heav'nly source,
   Strength to make you good and true,

Rise ev'ry morning just at six,
   And call your little brother,
Your clothes be sure you neatly fix,
   Then pray and help your mother.

Then, 'ere you do your breakfast take,
   Read verses in the Bible,
You scarce will feel a pain or ache
   Unless self is your idol.

Then set yourself a little task,
   Go then and do it brightly;
Speak kindly, and then gently ask,
   To bear your trials lightly.

Before each meal ask God to bless
   The food he has provided,
God loves those little children best
   Who by his hand are guided.

When the clock strikes one quickly run,
   And seat yourselves at table,
At dinner time just stop your fun,
   That is if you are able.

For if like angels we would live,
   And fit ourselves for glory,
We must our thoughts put through a seive,
   And daily grow more holy.

We must not let our bodies have
   Each wish, fancy or desire,
Or they will use up all our love,
   And our souls drop in the mire.

Whatever now your habits are,
   Each day they will grow stronger,
To make them good and regular,
   Our days will grow much longer.

TO MY NEPHEWS AND NIECES.

It seems to me I have nephews four,
And of little nieces just two more,
Now it really is my earnest wish,
That they to me should attentive list.

Begin at once good habits to make,
To conquer yourselves some measures take;
If your bodies are your only care,
Satan is sure your poor souls to snare.

First, they will ask that they shall be drest
In the very finest, very best,
No matter how it is to be got,
The contest may yet grow very hot.

Ev'ry one at you of course must stare
To see the fine things you have to wear,
But then if they really look, what gain,
What benefit, will it save you pain.

The body gets lazy when it's so fine,
For work or reading cannot find time;
Idleness opens the door to sin,
Whose web you will then begin to spin.

Of eating and drinking next beware,
For they often do mankind ensnare,
Every thing's good that God has given,
If but in moderation taken.

But appetite must be held in cheek,
Or it your bodies and souls will wreck,
As also your tongues be sure to tame,
Or you cannot earn a christ'an name.

Never be tempted to risk a cent,
On cards or games for amusement meant.
Innocent though in themselves they are,
When play'd for money they leave a scar.

Lotteries too are dangerous things,
Like fortune-telling they have their stings;
In those crooked and slippery ways,
Satan his flocks and his herds does graze.

Remember there is a wondrous mine,
Whose precious ore will your thoughts refine,—
One that contains the purest of gold,
Which will yield pleasures and joys untold.

If daily this treasure you explore
And draw from its vast exhaustless store,
The wisdom that God has hidden there,
To teach us which God his Son did spare.

When our lives reflect its glorious rays,
Gay, happy and bright will be our days;
New joys will over our senses steal,
Which Christ himself will to us reveal.

ON PHILATELY.

WRITTEN FOR A. E. M.

A book of stamps indeed
   For which a prize you sue,
All will at once concede
   That such is but your due.

To gather trifling things
   Requires much toil and care,
But labor's fairy wings
   Will hearts for truth prepare.

If those stamps could relate
   The sorrow, joy and pain,
The changes of estate,
   The merchandize and gain,

The learning and the lore,
   Both poesy and prose,
Which they from shore to shore
   Did one and all expose,

With wonder in our eyes
   We would scan their design,
And learn that little ties
   All nations do combine.

Great Britain, loyal, true,
   Her sovereign displays,
Most christian countries too
   Thus emulate her ways.

Some add to this a crown,
  While others have a shield,
Their coat of arms around,
  These stamps with pride are seal'd.

With numerals some place
  In shielded disk their arms,
With color change their face,
  Thus much enhance their charms.

An eagle, horse, and ram,
  The lion, unicorn,
Two bears erect like man,
  Various stamps do form.

A star on a bull's head
  Above a five and four,
With crown and eagle wed,
  And horn peace to restore.

A crown on eagle see,
  Laurel does it entwine;
The wings are open, free,
  This is a chaste design.

A castle on a rock—
  A stamp of weight indeed;
We only need to knock
  They will answer with speed.

Tiara and cross keys
  With some stars in a frame—
Many bend on their knees
  When these things we do name.

The Mahommedans seem
  To use things without life,
The moon we see there gleam
  With her reflected light.

The dragon in Shangai
  His figure does expose,
Pray, tell the reason why,
  If any body knows.

There among the heathen
  He moves along in peace,
But the Jew and Christian
  Will make his rule to cease.

St. George and this creature
  On Russian stamps behold,
But a brighter picture
  Beneath them does enfold—

For a sundial lays
  All ready down below,
To send forth some new rays,
  Which will pierce this our foe.

Egypt shows her learning,
  With geometric line;
Pyramids reminding
  Of that confusing time,

When God the race dispersed
  To all and every clime,
And when they first conversed
  By magic and by sign.

An orange tree appears,
  · Three post horns on its face—
All our hopes and our fears
  On this stamp we do place.

For when all in good tune
  Together they do blow,
Man and earth will assume
  Its mantle free from woe.

The stamp of truth will then
  On ev'ry face be seen,
Man's paradise again,
  All glorifi'd will gleam.

ANSWER WRITTEN ON HEARING THAT HE LOST THE PRIZE.

I grieve for you my little friend,
  As I see you did not gain
The prize for which you did contend,
  Though it seems you had a claim.

The reason why you lost the stamps
  Really now seems very plain,
Philately more from us demands
  Than your poem did contain.

It fail'd to notice places where
  The various stamps were sold,
To speak of those so very rare,
  Which we here and there behold.

But ignorance we here may plead:
  Both the Smith and Co.'s, you see,
Of Bath and Bristol fame indeed
  Were unknown to you and me.

Much money it appears is coin'd
  By selling a spur'ous kind,
Which from these firms has much purloind,
  Four circles do them define.

Concentric ones which postmen all
  Affix on the false design,
So each and all both great and small
  May easily learn the sign.

But oh there is a greater prize
    For which, when the Jews do aim,
We shall like gods become more wise,
    For Christ in our hearts will reign.

Our worship now is counterfeit,
    Four circles do it enclose;
Satan the human race does cheat,
    With his stamps all full of woes.

The stamp of truth he has effac'd
    With his crooked ways and means;
God's image with them is disgrac'd,
    So King death his harvest gleams

Help me to bring God's truth to light,
    You are sure to win a prize—
One that will daily grow more bright
    And more lovely in your eyes.

A crown you also will obtain,
    One that with this prize is sent.
O follow Christ in more than name,
    And truth, hope and love cement.

ON THE DEATH OF KELLY, WHO LOST HIS LIFE FROM FALLING FROM A NEW FIRE ESCAPE.

These great days of invention,
Do claim some attention,
For to benefit mankind,
To all danger men seem blind.

Kelly thus his life has lost,
Others with him felt its cost;
An escape made life to save,
Prov'd his pathway to the grave.

This steady, promising youth,
Ascended on it, forsooth,
To prove that now human skill,
High in air can mount at will.

Science making labor light
Most undoubtedly is right,
For the rich some daily task,
Soon will be forced to grasp.

Labor now is scarce and dear,
Useful things our hearts do cheer,
While all reckless, daring plans,
Surely some arrest demands.

Sudden deaths and accidents
Are such every day events,
That all heedlessly do say,
Well, we all must die some day.

Yet these changes, new and great,
Speak of some transition state;
Labor soon the world will rule,
For this we ourselves must school.

Money's power begins to wane,
Honest labor is to reign,
Dwelling each beneath his vine,
Love and duty will entwine.

Grain, the other ruling power,
Which we now call money's tower,
Will itself so much extend,
And will labor so befriend,

That a penny then will buy
More than pounds can now supply—
St. John did this to us reveal,
When the angel broke the seal.

Soon earth's Sabbath is to dawn,
Hail, with me, its beauteous morn;
Let each one at once prepare,
There is little time to spare.

So your lamps make haste and trim,
Quickly banish ev'ry sin,
When within us Christ does reign,
We will all have done with pain.

LINES WRITTEN ON BOARD THE STEAMER
AS SHE LEFT QUEBEC WHARF, SEPT., 1873.

Sitting on a boat at the wharf
Just as she's steaming to be off,
Levi ferry coming to port,
Glides in beneath the stately Fort.

Ships dotting all the coast around,
A man of War in centre found;
Row boats passing beneath our bows,
Steam whistles making their great rows.

Three River shoots at first ahead,
The market boats in turn have fled;
The mail boat follows in their wake
Bearing us all across the Lake.

Man and his works in constant stir —
Some wrapt in silk and some in fur.
Each with some selfish end to gain
Unwinding death's strong iron chain.

But round us all those hills and plains
Their quiet grandeur still maintains;
Nothing can move, nor can we reach,
But yet they us a lesson teach:

That strong and mighty is the Power
That guides us every day and hour,
Whose silent watch by day and night
Keeps every creature here in sight.

All are now working out his will,
His great designs we all fulfil;
Our actions well predestinate
The joys or woes that each await.

Each has the power some good to do,
But some will Evil still pursue.
Christ soon will all our ways amend
Then we will not our God offend.

AN INCIDENT OF THE 15TH NOV., 1873.

A story I to-day was told,
  When some aid I did implore,
By one who did withhold his gold,
  For my work he did deplore.

As useless, quite a waste of time,
  Which no good would ever do,
Its object christians to combine,
  Desirable, it is true.

But still a wild and foolish scheme,
  The breach very much too wide:
Why have you chosen such a theme?
  Pray set all such views aside.

For has not each a church to teach,
  And the Bible for their guide,
To such for any one to preach,
  Shows a great amount of pride.

So that we cannot tolerate,
  Nor in any way assist,
Your powers you much overrate,
  Pray at once I say, desist.

Monks, priests and friars all have failed
  Christianity to blend;
These Satan's kingdom have assailed,
  So you cannot gain your end.

The tale he did to me relate
  I will briefly here repeat,
For then it was I did checkmate,
  But he did not own defeat.

A preacher once of great renown
  Many conquests did achieve,
His fame was sounded through the town,
  Such a concourse did believe.

While really all the work was done
  By a friar on his knees,
His prayer the hearts of all had won—
  It is prayer that God does please.

This gives me hope at once, I said,
  I see how I can succeed;
My work will yet the churches wed,
  If all at Christ's throne will plead.

Then carefully peruse its leaves,
  When together they are bound,
You may find withs to bind the sheaves
  That now are scattered round.

And oh! do they not need to mate
  Is God's truth their glitt'ring pearl,
In our glorious future state,
  It will radiantly unfurl,

And shine upon each breast and face,
  So that all we do or say
Will leave a holy, heavenly trace,
  Pointing to eternal day.

Then Jews awake, my armour try,
  For you I have it prepar'd;
No longer ask the reason why,
  God to man his own Son spar'd.

IN MEMORIAM OF SIR GEORGE CARTIER.

What mournful pageant do I see,
  Marching with such measur'd pace?—
A body brought across the sea
  To find its last resting-place.

Sir George Cartier is his name,
  And a Statesman he has been;
Proudly he wore the crown of fame—
  Even kneeling to his Queen.

Why such pomp and ceremony?—
  It will never make amend
For grievous want of harmony
  Which hastened on his end.

Soldiers, Citizens and Priests,
  Drest out with such care and skill,
Take warning by this scene so *triste*—
  Guard, guide, and control your will.

A dazzling sight the Church was made,
  With its *Catafalque* so great;
But he who on it has been laid
  Cares no more for earthly state!

Those tapers, with their waning light,
  Remind us of earth's short day;
Why prize so much the things of sight?
  They but chase our souls away!

A Car, both elegant and grand,
   Now receives this box of clay;
In front his coat of arms does stand,
   And violet wreaths array.

The beauteous shamrock, thistle, rose,
   Together on it entwine;
But mother earth does now enclose
   To the tomb you did consign

This Senator you so respect,
   For his cheerful, honest way,
Who first did droop through your neglect,
   Upon that last voting day!

All creeds together now unite,
   For whate'er the flesh desires;
But every spiritual light
   Is still mix'd with earthly fires.

Or sin would not our peace destroy—
   Our bodies steal away—
Nor poison all our earthly joy,
   With its sickness and decay.

Let prejudice be cast aside,
   At once Christians combine,
To part with all that earthly pride
   Which mars God's great design!

A PRAYER.

Dear Father help, my spirit break,
In solitude it often aches;
Nothing can make men see or know,
No matter what I to them show.

That Christ must come as king to reign,
To banish sickness, death and pain.
Jew and Christian find it hard
To walk like Christ in virtue's garb.

Knowledge has taught them nature's laws
Must keep feeding Death's great jaws.
The earth would not mankind contain,
Unless Death did his part sustain.

This is the way they speak or think;
All seem to join in one great link.
Alone on earth I really stand,
Assailed by strife on every hand.

But surely thou, who madest man—
Who the whole universe did span—
Can make the earth our Paradise,
And banish all and ev'ry vice.

Our senseless idols all can change,
Our lifeless images derange;
Can give our spirits endless life,
And make an end of all our strife,

Unite us then with holy love;
Our Faith awaken from above;
Fit us to serve and worship thee,
The great and Mighty One and Three.

The mind of man with study great
Knows little of his great estate;
How few can all the birds define,
And class them in their native clime.

Then look at ev'ry tree and flower
Changing their color day and hour,
Their names are legion; in each zone,
How many various kinds are known.

But, like the rainbow in the sky,
Their lovely hues live but to die;
And none can really comprehend
The light that does them all transcend.

O make the human mind expand,
Thy mysteries to understand,
Give us the wisdom we require,
And feed us with electric fire.

2ND PART.

Then teach me, teach me Lord, I pray,
How I can thy work array,
That it may draw the Jew to thee,
At thy cross to bend the knee.

To make them feel thou hast been here
All our hearts with love to cheer,
To teach them that thy power so great
Chose to come in low estate.

The Evil one so well ensnares,
Hearts so fills with earthly cares,
That words like mine they do not prize,
For its truths their spirit tries.

But if God's truth it does contain
He my efforts will sustain,
And, in spite of all men's pride,
Will disperse it far and wide.

Pray, Esau's sons, come chaff the wheat,
Draw Christ from his Heav'nly seat,
Search with me his precious mine,
And with glory earth will shine.

Come humbly to the throne of grace,
Worship him who fills all space
With faith and love, a small return
Which Christ left his throne to earn.

Pride is the Evil one's delight,
For it dims our spirit's sight;
Like children try to learn and trust
That God's plan is wise and just.

The veil must rise from off your eyes
Before Jesus you can prize,
And earth can never Heaven become
Till your homage Christ has won.

Then let me urge, yes, beg, entreat,
That your people all will greet
The treasures dug from God's own mine,
Which within this volume shine.

Then making trial of its truth,
By imparting it to youth,
So that the glory it portrays
May be brought within our gaze.

For when we act and think aright,
New joys will our souls delight,
And with the countless angel throng
We will mingle heart and song.

THE ROUND CHURCH.

THE ROUND CHURCH.

When I walk around this lovely city,
   And see the churches so new and so grand,
I cannot help thinking 'tis a pity
   That Christians are a divided band.

When to Sinai's plains all mankind repair'd,
   One speech and one language they entertain'd;
To build a tower they their bricks prepar'd,
   Whose top should reach heav'n, but God restrain'd.

The Lord descended and scatter'd men round,
   Confounded their language and changed their plan;
But the Evil Spirit has always found
   New works, new schemes for his enemy man.

To the Jewish altar in glory God came,
   And gently and kindly bid him obey,
His own way he chose, his will would not tame,
   Year past after year, obey would not they.

Then Prophets He sent His will to declare,
   Priests He desired His work to fulfil;
His Son, next He spared a way to prepare,
   He suffered, He died, man disobeys still.

This beautiful world in six days he made,
   Fit place for angels till Satan appeared,
A plan of Redemption for us God laid,
   A Temple quite round He'll cause to be reared.

Whose praises and prayers to God will ascend,
   United in heart, in soul and in mind;
A ray from God's throne will on it descend,
   And comfort and rest the world will there find.

Then Oh, once again, man united will be,
   The spirit of goodness comes to restore ;
Yes, when he comes he will make evil flee,
   Encircle the Temple with graces three.

When it is built and man worships in Love,
   When his Faith in his works shine all round,
The Lord will descend, will come from above,
   And then every thing good will abound.

JEWS AND CHRISTIANS.

As perhaps our first pure Holy Catholic Church may be a round one, I have thought it well to embellish my book with a plate of St. Sepulchre's Round Church, Cambridge, which is one of the four round Churches still remaining in the Kingdom of Great Britain. This one at Little Maplestead in Essex was dedicated to St. John of Jerusalem and given to the Templars by Juliana wife of William, Son of Anderlin, steward to Henry II. It was customary during the Crusades to build Parish Churches in honor of the Holy Sepulchre, hence the origin of its name, and the parish in which it was built was called the Jewry: this arose from the foolish idea that it was once a Jewish Synagogue and that the Jews lived there. It is supposed to have been erected in the reign of Henry 1st, between the first and second Crusades, and to be the oldest church of its form in England. As this date is but a very few years after the order of Templars, it was probably not built by them, but it might afterwards have got into their possession by gift; and when the order was dissolved in the year 1313 the advowson was given to the priory of Barnwell, at which time it has been supposed the tower was raised a story higher for the reception of bells—the chancel being then added and dedicated to St. Andrew the Patron of Barnwell Priory. The circular part of the church is 41 feet in diameter. The writer is indebted to a friend for the sketch of the church and its history, and has placed it in this book with the hope that round churches fed by five streams of Sacramental Grace from our Saviour's wounds, with doors well closed against Satan's devices, will like beacon lights draw all men unto them, and that the knowledge they will impart will make each household a place from which will ascend daily offerings of prayer and praise so that God will be worshipped in the hearts and homes of his people as also in his house with a pure and hearty devotion. The labor of years, which has been a work of love, the writer now submits to your earnest consideration, sincerely believing that God will remove the curse of sin when we all together fulfil his righteous will, for he has so said in the following and numerous other passages, " Be still and know that I am God. I will be exalted among the heathen, I will be exalted on the earth."—Psalm 46.

In his days shall the righteous flourish : and abundance of peace so long as the moon endureth."—Psalm lxxii. 7.

It shall come to pass in the last days that the mountain of the Lord's house shall be established in the mountains, and shall be exalted above the hills, and all nations shall flow unto it.—Isaiah 2,

He will swallow up death in victory, and the Lord God will wipe away tears from off all faces, and the rebuke of his people shall he take away from off the earth, for the Lord hath spoken it.—Isaiah 25.

THE BIBLE.

THE BIBLE.

This book containing all God's will,
  His gift from heaven to man;
The evil spirit has, and still
  Declares to be a sham

Give your proof, the atheist cries
  That it from God did come;
For ev'ry church and sect now tries
  To call itself the one

That knows and understands God's word,
  That can its truths portray;
Each one the voice of God has heard,
  And claims Christ for his stay.

The Jew believes the first five books,
  And trusts the prophets too;
But in the Gospel never looks,
  For Christ they never knew.

A stumbling block we are to them,
  With our divided views;
O, that the labour of my pen
  Would christianize the Jews.

For they will all of us unite,
  God they both love and fear;
When they acknowledge Christ with might,
  All will be plain and clear.

Then atheists and heathens, all
  Will learn to know the Lord;
The scales from off their eyes will fall,
  They'll say he was the word

Who faithfully fulfilled the law,
    And taught us how to live,
Who, the inspired prophets saw,
    And God to earth did give.

The great love that our God has shown,
    Will then strike sinners dumb,
God's word will then on earth be known,
    And all will hail God's Son.

The first three chapters shew how sin
    Brought death on all mankind,
The last three teach us that our kin,
    The Tree of Life will find.

When God does in his temple reign,
    In every heart supreme;
Our bodies freed from death and pain,
    All glorified will gleam.

Now let us scan its books to see
What our God's design can be,
In condescending to impart
To his creatures, any chart.

GENESIS.

Genesis, the first streak of light
That Moses, God's scribe did write;
Informs us of our origin,
And our loss of life through sin.

Six days of labour God proclaimed,
Adam's work he then ordained;
God bid him Eden dress and keep,
Ere he laid him down to sleep.

And told him to keep the Sabbath day
In a blessed, holy way;
To worship Him, the Holy One,
Who the thread of life has spun.

Then when God Adam disobeyed,
Satan having him betrayed,
The race were all condemned to die,
Evil dimmed man's lovely eye.

A scheme of mercy to restore,
Life to give us evermore;
God did Himself for us design,
Through His Son, the living vine.

As Adam's seed grew worse and worse,
God to Noah did converse.
And told him he would sweep away
Nearly all this worthless clay.

An ark, God then bid Noah frame,
His own household to contain;
While with water He did baptize
Earth which so his spirit tries.

Again mankind did multiply,
And united they did try
A tow'r or church to try and make,
With stairs to lead to heav'n's gate.

Such human stairs, then God did say,
Shall not open heaven's way.
Their languages I shall confuse,
For my mercies they abuse.

Abram, the true and faithful priest,
Now stands out in bold relief;
His call and promise that his seed,
To God's favor man will lead.

Melchizedek, the king divine,
Blessed him with bread and wine;
Our sacred feast we here behold,
First began in days of old.

To their own land Jews will return·
When they one and all discern
That Christ was the Messiah true,
Who will man and earth renew.

When they accept the sacrifice,
The life, death and blood of Christ;
As the substitute which was slain,
Man to save from future pain.

He for mankind does intercede,
For our future welfare plead;
His spirit tries to hold a check,
And with virtues us to deck.

This people such great love obtained
Through the faith Abram sustained;
When told to sacrifice his child,
He at once agreed, complied.

He did not ask the reason why
His dear son, so young must die?'
But took the knife at once to slay,
When the angel bid him stay.

That gentle son we must revere,
Who without a doubt or fear,
When Abram took him up on high,
Did at once prepare to die.

The sacrifice before prepar'd,
Suddenly to them appear'd;
The angel to the altar led
The ram, which they slew instead.

Abraham in this scene did see
Christ upon th' accursed tree;
Then he rejoic'd to see the day
That taught him the heav'nly way.

But yet again, he mourns and sighs,
His dear wife before him dies;
Land he buys from the sons of Heth,
That she may repose in death.

There liv'd but Isaac of his race,
To fulfil the law of grace;
Through him he knew, God did decree,
Man from sin to set quite free.

The blessings promis'd to his seed,
He did now believe indeed;
So Isaac's wife must be procur'd,
His descendants here secur'd.

His servant quickly forth he sent,
To his kinsmen's house he went;
A wife for Isaac to secure,
One who was both good and pure.

Rebekah met him at the well,
She ran home his tale to tell,
And shew the presents he had brought
To deck her, the bride he sought.

The hand of God in this they saw,
And with them, his will was law;
So at once they gave consent,
And Rebekah forthwith went

To meet the one she was to wed,
Straight was she to Isaac led;
The servant told what he had done,
She the love of Isaac won.

To Sarah's tent he took his bride,
In her place she did preside,
Spreading around a lustrous light,
Like a good and faithul wife.

The promised heir did not appear,
Till he reached his three-score year,
Rebekah then had two twin boys,
Thus did God complete their joys.

The Lord had to Rebekah said,
When her mind was full of dread,
Two sons will soon delight your eyes,
From whom nations will arise.

Two nations from them must have sprung,
For God's word is surely done ;
A yoke the younger was to twine,
Round the elder for a time.

Esau the elder soon became
The great hunter of the plain,
While Jacob dwelt within his tent,
Sodding pottage was his bent.

One day when Esau home returned,
Hunger sore within him burned,
For this red pottage he did sell
His birthright to hill and dell.

This son at forty years of age,
Did two heathen wives engage,
Causing his parents grief of mind—
Thus his future yoke did bind.

For his mother it did estrange,
So the plan she did arrange,
Of dressing Jacob in a skin,
When he did the blessing win.

This Yoke will Esau's nation break,
When in Faith they all partake
Of the Holy Fire in the bread,
And wine on the altar spread.

What Jacob won by treach'rous means,
Drove him off to foreign scenes,
From Esau he is forced to fly,
For he vows that he shall die.

To Bethuel's house he wends his way,
Walking on till close of day,
Some stones for pillows he does pile,
When to rest he does recline.

Lonely and weary soon he sleeps,
Tears may have bedewed his cheeks.
He dreams he sees a ladder set,
On which he may to Heaven get.

Angels on it did come and go,
They the way already know;
The Lord himself above it stood,
He, the great, the wise, the good.

Said, like the dust thy seed shall be,
This land now I give to thee;
Through thee shall all the earth be blessed,
And spread round from east to west.

Thy footsteps I will guide aright,
And be to thee a shining light;
To this land thou shalt yet return,
And in it thou shalt sojourn.

Jacob awaking from his dream,
Felt that God did reign supreme,
His stone pillow he there set up,
Pouring oil upon the top.

The place he then did Bethel name,
And aloud he did exclaim,
God's house this stone shall surely be,
For the gate of Heaven I see.

Then Jacob vow'd to God a vow,
Being overcome with awe,
That if God would him guard and guide,
And for all his wants provide,

When he again in peace return'd,
Of whatever he had earn'd
A tenth to God he would restore,
Praising him for evermore.

Onward he on his journey went,
Eastward he his footsteps bent,
When some score of miles did divide
Him from his native fireside.

He saw reclining in a dell,
Three flocks of sheep round a well,
Waiting for Laban's flocks to come—
Watering had not begun.

Then to the shepherd he did say,
Know ye Laban up this way,
Yes, we know him, he liveth here,
And his daughter draweth near.

Upon the well a great stone lay,
Which Jacob did roll away,
When Rachel came with Laban's sheep,
Kissing her he then did weep,

Saying he was Rebekah's son.
She at once did homeward run,
How much amazed she must have been,
Now, how chang'd to her the scene.

When Laban heard his daughter's tale,
He his sister's son did hail
With a welcome cheerful and kind,
And for wages did him bind.

Now Laban's heart this news made glad,
For he two fine daughters had,
Rachel and Leah were their names,
Kindred then had marriage claims.

The wages were fair Rachel's hand,
He of Laban did demand,
Seven years to serve him he agreed,
All his flocks and herds to feed.

When these seven years had expired,
Jacob of Laban desired
His youngor daughter for his wife,
For he lov'd her as his life.

But Laban Jacob did deceive,
Giving him, another Eve,
Who was Leah his eldest child,
She that was the tender-eyed.

He serv'd him other seven years,
In this narrative appears,
For Rachel his beloved 's sake,
And increased in glory great.

When to Rachel a son was born
He again did Laban warn,
That he his service then should leave—
Laban still to him did cleave.

A new agreement then was made
That in herds he should be paid—
The speckled and the spotted ones
Jacob's property becomes.

When mighty grew his flocks and herds
Jealousy made angry words,
The time had come for them to part,
So in secret he did start.

To his home on his native shore
Where he once in days of yore
His brother Esau did betray,
When with skin he did array.

The third day after Jacob fled
Laban with his brethren sped,
For seven days they did pursue
Ere he did appear in view.

Then Laban's anger passed away,
For the Lord in dream did say:
Speak not to Jacob good or ill,
Thus did God control his will.

Still they did meet with war of words,
Caus'd from loss of flocks and herds,
For Laban said all thine is mine,
Then a covenant they did sign.

They gather'd stones into a heap,
On the top of them did eat,
Laban gave them Chaldean name,
Jacob Hebrew, but the same.

Mizpah, or Beacon let it be,
To give light to you and me,
A sacrifice they there did make,
And of bread they did partake.

They tarried on the mount all night;
Early in the morning light
Laban his children did caress,
And departing also bless.

As Jacob now went on his way
Angels shed a holy ray,
Heaven hosts did him surround
As he march'd along the ground.

Still when to Esau he draws near
He is much distress'd with fear,
Instead of yielding to despair
He uplifts his heart in prayer.

Then bands of cattle he does send
As a present, to amend
For that great blessing which he won
From him, Isaac's eldest son.

His prayers ascended up on high,
Brought Jehovah from the sky,
Gave Jacob power to prevail,
Satan's Kingdom to assail.

His brother's anger did appease,
When seven times he bowed his knees,
Then Esau met him and embrac'd,
And receiv'd his gifts with grace.

They parted now quite reconcil'd,
At Schekem the long exil'd,
Another altar did erect—
This one, though, God did reject,

Because his children had done wrong,
Having slain the great and strong,
When he was overwhelmed with woe,
God bid him on to Bethel go.

Then his household he did command,
On their leaving Schekem's Land,
Their idols each and all to hide,
Beneath an oak, side by side,

Again the Lord appeared to him,
When he put away this sin,
Desiring him to change his name,
In view of much greater fame.

For multiply God said he should,
And the ground on which he stood,
He gave to Abram and his seed.
It should all be theirs indeed.

Of stones a pillar he did pile,
Streaming down upon them oil;
A drink offering he then did pour
Out of his abundant store.

Then God his servant Jacob tries,
Rachel his beloved dies,
But though his wife from him is torn,
Unto him a son is born.

Thus death and life we see combined,
And to each a place assigned,
Just as Christ's body for us died,
That we should be justified.

Sending his spirit life to give,
That hereafter we may live,
Like Jesus pure and without guile,
Free from all that can defile.

When this spiritual reign begins,
We will vanquish Satan's sins;
Decay and death will not then spoil,
All our labour and our toil.

PART THE SECOND.

The sacred writer further states,
That Jacob again migrates
With his great and mighty band
To Hebron, his father's land.

Then Isaac old and full of days,
The sad debt of nature pays,
Esau and Jacob him inter
In his father's sepulchre.

The brothers now do separate,
Because they are so rich and great,
That they cannot together dwell,
So they part and say farewell.

In Edom Esau spread his tent,
When from Canaan's land he went,
Great dukes and princes from him sprung,
And Priest Reul was his son.

He was the first who bore the name,
This Priest of Midian's plain,
His seven daughters, we are told,
Brought the sheep into the fold.

One of them Moses' heart did win,
When he fled from Egypt's King,
So Zipporah forthwith he wed,
And a shepherd's life he led.

But Jacob dwelt in Canaan's land,
With twelve sons at his right hand ;
Joseph and Benjamin he lov'd,
All the other sons above.

These were his own dear Rachel's sons,
They were his most cherish'd ones.
For Joseph a fine coat was made,
With colours of every shade.

His brethren then did jealous grow,
Soon they did their envy show ;
He dreams two dreams which seem to prove
He above them yet should move.

These did arouse their pride and hate,
They said he should not be great ;
Reign over them, he never should,
Thus together they did brood.

While feeding of their fathers' flocks,
Satan whispering thus knocks,
When poor young Joseph does appear,
Sent by Israel he draws near.

Together they agree to slay
A beast devour'd we will say,
But Reuben said, Thou shalt not kill,
His blood we must never spill.

Into a pit they had him cast,
When some Ishmalites went past;
They decided it would be well,
To these people him to sell.

Then twenty silver pieces they
For him did agree to pay,
And with them to Egyptian ground
Joseph as a slave was bound.

To Potiphar these traders sold
This young man again for gold,
His overseer he then became,
Till his wife did falsely blame.

Then into prison he was thrust,
But as he was wise and just,
The keeper put into his care,
The prisoners and their fare.

Two servants did the King offend,
To this prison he did send,
It seems, the captain of the guard
Assigned both to Joseph's ward.

Now each of these men had a dream:
They were sighing for a gleam
Of what it did to them portend,
Fearing it foretold their end,

When Joseph brought their morning meal,
And their meaning did reveal,
For he was spiritually wise,
Because he God's laws did prize.

The butler in his dream did see
A great vine with branches three,
Which buds and blossoms did produce,
And fine grapes for Pharoah's use.

King Pharoah's cup he did behold,
And in his own hand did hold;
He press'd the grapes into the cup,
Then to Pharoah gave it up.

The meaning Joseph did him give,
Was that he again should live
In King Pharoah's mansion great,
Three days would him reinstate.

Then, when with thee all things go well,
My sad story you can tell;
In prison I should not remain,
For no crime my soul does stain.

But stolen from my Hebrew home,
I am in this land alone;
With no one here to plead for me,
Or to try to set me free.

The baker then his dream relates,
In the hope some good awaits;
Such as Joseph had just foretold,
The king's butler should be told.

Upon my head three baskets white,
With bake meats above in sight;
While birds did eat them from my head,
Though for Pharoah they were spread.

In three days thou shalt cease to be,
Hanging then upon a tree;
The birds shall peck thy flesh away,
This is what thy dream doth say.

And each of these men met the fate
Joseph said did them await;
To celebrate the king's birthday,
Life and death they did portray.

The prison gates did open wide,
And they came out side by side;
The baker to be hang'd was sent,
Joyful forth the other went

To dwell again in Pharoah's hall,
And to answer to his call;
Joseph's release he never sought,
On him he did cast no thought,

Till at the end of two full years,
In dream to the king appears
Seven fat-flesh'd and full-favor'd kine,
Which in meadow did recline,

When seven ill-favor'd and quite lean
Soon appear upon the scene;
The fat, the lean ones food supplies,
They devour before his eyes.

Another dream his senses chain,
For he wakes and sleeps again;
Seven rank and good ears of corn,
To one stalk seem hanging on.

When seven thin and blasted ears
Suddenly to him appears;
These, the good ones do soon devour,
For like evil, they had pow'r.

In the morn the king sat in state,
With magicians wise and great;
In vain he did to them appeal,
They could not his dreams reveal.

Then the butler recall'd to mind
Joseph once to him so kind,
And to the king he did repeat
Where he did with Joseph meet,

And how truly he did explain
Dreams which gave his servants pain;
The king for Joseph forthwith sent,
To interpret what was meant

By his two dreams, none could define,
Though he felt they were a sign;
Which some great trouble did portend,
And to which he should attend.

At once from prison he did call
This man, wise above them all;
In haste he does himself array,
And to Pharoah wend his way.

His dreams to him he now does state,
His uneasiness was great;
You can interpret them they say,
Quickly do so then I pray

With help from the God I fear.
I will make it plain and clear;
For we can nothing truly know,
But what God does to us show.

The kine and corn are both the same,
The one meaning will explain:
The kine so good that you did see,
Seven plentiful years to be.

u

The lean and blasted are to show
Seven years when nought shall grow;
A'fifth part of the plenty ears,
You must gather, it appears,

That for the famine long and sore,
You may have an ample store;
To carry out this enterprise,
Find a man discreet and wise,

And place him over Egypt's land,
All the corn at his command,
With officers who shall provide,
And a fifth part set aside.

That when the seven good years are past,
Your corn may be made to last
Till those seven sad years are fled,
Which all now have cause to dread.

So Joseph rose to glory great
Second only in estate
To Pharoah Egypt's Mighty King
To him all the corn they bring.

And to Joseph the king did say,
All to thee shall homage pay;
My signet-ring I give to thee,
Thou shalt my great ruler be.

Array'd in beauteous linen white
With pure golden chain in sight,
Thou shalt in a chariot ride,
A priest's daughter for your bride.

For God's spirit in you does shine,
Wisdom round you does entwine;
As you have warn'd, so you will save
From a sad, untimely grave.

While Joseph gather'd up the corn,
Unto him two sons were born;
Ephraim and Manasseh nam'd,
He chief ruler was proclaim'd.

To Pharoah all the people ran
When the years of dearth began;
He did to Joseph them commend,
Bidding them to him attend,

For he would in this crisis guide,
His storehouses open wide;
For corn enough they did contain,
All his people to maintain.

This famine spread itself around,
Hard and sterile was the ground;
Egypt alone had corn in store,
Thanks to Joseph and his lore.

So Joseph's brethren thither went,
By their father Jacob sent,
That they might corn for him procure,
For much want they did endure.

These ten who Joseph had betray'd
See this ruler well array'd;
But never dream he is the one
That their sin should bid them shun.

To him they throw themselves prostrate,
And their wants at once relate;
He sees in them his treach'rous foes,
They the cause of all his woes.

He says with anger in his eyes,
Well I know that you are spies;
Our barren fields you come to see,
That, I tell you must not be.

Then they quickly to him reply,
No! we do not come to spy,
We are twelve sons of one man, true,
All of whom are here but two.

The youngest we did leave at home,
One is not, to this we own:
Till I have proof of what you say,
Here you must in prison stay.

Three days in ward they did remain
Ere their object they did gain;
Then corn in plenty Joseph sends,
Treating these his foes, as friends.

But Simeon he does retain,
Causing them much grief and pain;
Till they return, and with them bring
Their young brother Benjamin.

Each finds his money in his sack,
When to Canaan they got back;
This fills their mind with awe and fear,
When to Jacob they draw near.

They to their father do return,
Telling him of their sojourn;
He mourns and says, you me bereave,
Why do thus my children leave.

Joseph gone, Simeon away,
Benjamin he wants, you say;
He is my very dearest one,
No, you cannot have this son.

Then Reuben to his father prays,
But he heeds not what he says;
He offers his two sons in trust,
For to Egypt go he must.

The subject was again resum'd,
When their corn was all consum'd.
Jacob said go again and buy
Corn for us before we die.

So Judah spake to him and said,
Egypt's ruler we much dread;
He said when you return for corn,
Bring me back thy youngest born,

That I may feel that you are true,
And a shepherd's life pursue—
He seem'd to think that we were spies,
And that all we said were lies.

I will be surety for the lad;
To want food is very sad,
On me for ever be the blame,
If you do not him reclaim.

Consent at last the father gave,
Saying, him from danger save,
The grave my body will receive,
If of him you me bereave.

Then laden well with fruits and spice,
And of other things the choice,
With double money in their hand,
Off they start corn to demand.

And when to Joseph they appear'd,
That great man they so much fear'd,
Seeing again his brother dear,
Scarcely could restrain a tear.

Together we shall dine to-day,
He to them at once did say;
To Joseph's house they then were led
When they had their asses fed.

They forthwith to the steward spake,
For with dread they now did shake,
Double money pray now receive,
To our sacks our gold did cleave.

But he quickly to them replied:
God your sacks with gold supplied,
Here is Simeon you left behind,
Keep the treasure you did find.

As soon as Joseph home did come,
On their knees themselves they flung;
Thus bowing down they did fulfil
Dreams which envy did instil.

Your father, is his health still good,
An old man I understood?
They reply, he is yet alive,
And this is his youngest child.

When to Benjamin he drew near,
His own mother's son so dear,
With love his heart did overflow,
So a blessing did bestow.

To hide the tears upon his cheek,
He did then his chamber seek;
But for a time he must restrain,
Even though it gave him pain.

Bidding his servants set on bread,
He return'd to see them fed;
Each according to his birthright,
Sat around his board in sight.

He messes from before him sent,
Each one according to descent;
But to the youngest, dearest one,
Five times greater was the sum.

Then Joseph bid his steward put
In the youngest's sack his cup,
And in the others what they paid
On the top should there be laid.

They early rose and sped away,
Almost at the dawn of day,
But Joseph's steward them o'ertook,
For his cup to search and look.

He did them all accuse and say,
Why take Joseph's cup away,
The one with which he does divine,
And from which he takes his wine.

This accusation they deny,
Then they all do him defy,
And beg that he will call to mind,
Gold they in their sacks did find.

And which they did to him return,
Aught to steal they all would spurn,
In any sack should it be found,
To my Lord we will be bound.

And he must die who did it steal,
His life such an act should seal.
The sacks are search'd, their hearts must burn,
Benjamin awaits his turn.

Lo! in his sack the cup they find,
Fear and sorrow fill their mind.
When Joseph's house they all do reach,
Bowing down they him beseech.

Joseph then met them, it does say,
Saying, in decided way,
What deed is this that you have done,
Now I claim this youngest son.

As my servant he shall remain,
The rest I will not detain.
Knew you not that I could divine,
When you took that cup of mine.

Then Judah said, keep me I pray,
This youth must not, cannot stay;
Our father's heart will surely break,
If his home he does forsake.

I am the surety for the lad,
He one brother only had,
Who from his home has stray'd away,
I for him am bound to stay.

Then let me to your mind recall,
That you told us, one and all,
To bring this youth when we did come,
Or you all of us would shun.

My father the old man will die
If you do not hear my cry;
In mercy this from you I crave,
Save, oh! save him, from the grave.

This pleading was not all in vain,
Joseph could no more refrain;
He bid his servants from him go,
While he made his brothers know

He was the one that they had sold
Into Egypt's land for gold;
That the trials he had endur'd
Peace and plenty had secur'd.

He to his brethren then did say:
Come quite near to me I pray,
I am Joseph whom ye did sell,
Grieve not for now all is well.

God sent me here corn to provide,
Through the famine all to guide;
To preserve life in this fair land,
God has plac'd me in command.

My father, go and bring with haste,
See that you no time do waste;
Tell him that Joseph bids him come,
Egypt's lord is his own son.

To bring his children, flocks and herds,
Say that these are Joseph's words,
In Goshen he must come and dwell,
I will there maintain him well.

All my glory to him relate,
In this kingdom I am great:
He with his brothers then did weep.
Kissing each upon the cheek.

Their cruelty he thus forgave,
And Christlike their lives did save.
We see in him the type of One,
Who for us has borne the sum.

Of God's great wrath to guilty man,
And when all accept his plan,
He leaves his mansions in the sky,
Man and earth to glorify.

A greater Joseph far than he,
In *Thee*, Saviour, I see;
Thou hast plenty of corn in store,
Come and open out the door.

The famine now begins to dawn,
Sell to Esau's sons thy corn;
Thy Church in glory they'll array,
Though they once did thee betray.

Thy doctrine they will all entwine,
When they know thou art Divine;
Thy Christian virtues all display,
And to thee such homage pay.

That heathen nations far and near,
In thy Temple will appear,
And spread thy sacred holy feast
In the countries of the East.

Thy cup containing purest wine,
Drawn from thee the living vine,
Will cleanse and purify our souls—
To our lips be as live coals.

The Temple which was rent in twain,
When our sins Christ did sustain,
Will be cemented well with love,
And the Spirit, like the dove,

Will on the altar spread his wings
Like the former Cherubims,
And God's own great and wondrous light,
Will again appear in sight.

The fame of Joseph's brethren sped,
And new lustre on him shed;
Then Pharoah unto him did say,
Wagons send for them I pray.

Your father and his household all,
Young and old, the great and small,
Must come and dwell in Egypt's Land,
All the best they can command.

Asses laden with corn and bread,
As the King to him had said,
With many other things as good,
He to Jacob sent for food.

Changes of raiment did present
To his brethren ere they went,
Five changes to the youngest one,
And a very handsome sum.

To Canaan they did wend their way,
And to Jacob they did say:
Joseph thy son is yet alive,
And in Egypt he does thrive,

As Governor he rules the land.
This he could not understand,
He seemed to fear they did deceive,
His heart could not this believe.

But when they told him Joseph's words,
Bidding him, with flocks and herds,
To Goshen, go and there to dwell,
Truth he knew they did him tell.

His spirit in him did revive,
Hearing Joseph was alive;
See him he must before he dies,
So to him at once he flies.

As he his journey does pursue,
He stops to give God his due;
His offerings reach his throne above,
And he answers him in love.

Fear not, he says, go on your way,
I will guard and be thy stay;
A nation great shall spring from thee,
Joseph you again shall see.

He and seventy of his seed
On this journey did proceed,
At Goshen Joseph did him meet,
And upon his neck did weep.

Then to Pharoah he did explain,
That they all from Canaan came,
As shepherds they had always been,
Their flocks they had brought to glean.

Egyptians scorn'd a shepherd's life,
So, perhaps in dread of strife,
In Goshen they did all remain,
Spreading round o'er all the plain.

Five of his brethren he did bring,
And present unto the King,
His father also Joseph brought,
And King Pharoah's favor sought.

What his your age, the King did say,
Jacob tell me now I pray?
Six score and ten years I have seen,
Few and evil they have been.

King Pharoah then did Jacob bless.
Joseph gave him to possess
The best of land in Ramases,
Where his mind would be at ease.

And with the very best of fare,
Nourish'd all his kin with care ;
Though the famine was very sore,
Never failing was their store.

Money and cattle, herds and lands,
Egyptians placed in Joseph's hands,
For he alone had corn for sale—
Without corn death must prevail.

When the sad seven years were past
He foretold the dearth should last,
They sought him that they might procure
Seed that would good crops ensure.

Then Joseph to them all did say,
For seed I buy you to-day,
A fifth of the corn you agree,
Pharoah's shall in future be.

The people with one voice declare
He had kept them from despair,
Yes, he had saved a nation's lives
Through his wondrous enterprise.

At once this scheme they all embrace
Thus he bought up all the race,
A fifth from them he should obtain
As a right the king would claim.

In Egypt's land here, it appears,
Jacob lived for seventeen years,
Then feeling that the time drew nigh
That he must prepare to die,

He called for Joseph to consent
That his body should be sent
To his father's burying place,
There to rest with his own race,

That altogether they might rise
To obtain their Heav'nly prize.
Yes, Abram, Isaac, Jacob all,
There will hear the angel's call.

The angel that Jews now reject,
Is the one they may expect;
When he returns his own to free,
Their Messiah they will see.

The Spirit now my pen employs
To remind you of the joys
That God will on his people pour,
When the time of trial's o'er.

Then all, with cheerful heart and voice,
That have made God's Truth their choice
Shall meet the Saviour in the air,
With the angels bright and fair.

Seven score and seven was Jacob's age
When he vanished from earth's stage;
He grew infirm, his eye grew dim,
Ere he paid the debt of sin.

When on his deathbed he was laid,
He to his son Joseph said:
The blessings God bestowed on me
I now give to thine and thee.

Some pages of Scripture show
That on him he did bestow
The land where God to him appear'd,
When through virtue's paths he steer'd.

Joshua says that Joseph's land
Bethel's altar did command;
St. John describes to us Jacob's well,
Near Sychar in Joseph's dell.

'Tis plain, what Jacob most did prize
He did give at his demise
To Joseph, with the prophecy
That his seed should occupy

It, at some far off distant time,
Thus fulfilling God's design,
That Abram's seed should reinstate
Christ on earth in glory great.

He now his other sons does call,
To tell them what shall befall
Each of their Tribes in future days,
Just according to their ways.

Reuben, thou my power and might,
Parted with what was thy right,
By falling into Satan's snare,
Which he for thee did prepare.

Simeon and Levi's cruelty
Caused a sad atrocity—
In their anger they did betray,
Yes, and afterwards did slay.

These through the earth shall be dispersed,
For their anger they were cursed;
Like Reuben, sin did in them dwell,
So they never can excel.

To Judah all the rest must bend,
On him they must all attend,
For Shiloh from him should appear,
Gathering from far and wear.

Those whose garments in blood washed white,
Will appear to claim their right;
To enjoy pure and happy days,
Learning more of wisdom's ways.

Our Shiloh has from Judah sprung,
Jesus from that Tribe did come,
All these his own did him disown,
Still he is to them unknown.

God's sceptre they do still maintain,
And to Moses' laws lay claim;
When they in Christ their Shiloh see,
Earth will a pure Eden be.

Zebulon shall a haven be,
Bordering upon the sea,
Issacher, like a couching ass,
Must pay tribute as a class.

Dan was crafty and serpentlike,
From the rear would always strike;
A warlike troop from Gad should spring,
Which to order he should bring.

Asher shall of the best partake,
Royal dainties he shall make.
Swift as a hind is Naphtali,
With good words his way will ply.

How sorely Joseph thou wert tried,
But with strength thou wert supplied;
Thy father's blessing did prevail,
When temptation did assail.

Thou art really a goodly tree,
Very fruitful shalt thou be;
Many great blessings shall descend,
And around thy paths attend.

Benjamin thou wilt seize thy prey,
Like a wolf at peep of day;
At night the spoil you will divide
With the members of your tribe.

And with these blessings Jacob said,
Bury me when I am dead,
Within the cave in Abram's field,
Then his life to God did yield.

Joseph his father did embrace,
Shedding tears upon his face;
The brothers must have all withdrawn,
He alone is there to mourn.

The body now must be embalmed,
And so when his sorrow calmed,
The physician he desires
To arrange as it requires.

Forty days did his mourning last;
Then we read when these were past,
That he did from the King demand
Time to go to Canaan's land,

His father's body to inter
In the very sepulchre
Where Abraham and Isaac lie,
Which these ancestors did buy.

Then Pharoah gave them leave to go,
He had sworn it must be so;
His servants, elders he did send,
With his own they him attend

This long and mournful cavalcade
Seven days at Atab stayed
Ere they proceeded on their way,
Jacob's mandate to obey.

Their work performed, they all return,
And in Egypt they sojourn;
But Joseph's brethren are in dread,
As their father now is dead,

That Joseph will their sin repay,
So they send to beg and pray
That he will not their sins recall,
But forgive them one and all.

Joseph sweetly to them replies,
With tears flowing from his eyes,
To save much people was I sent,
God wrought good from ill intent.

Be comforted and never fear,
You and yours to me are dear;
I will nourish them and thee,
From this sin I set you free.

v

In course of time Joseph expir'd :
Like his father he desir'd
That to Canaan he be convey'd
In his father's tomb be laid.

EXODUS.

That generation passed away,
Pharoah nature's debt did pay,
So fruitful had Israel become
That Egypt they overrun.

Another king now did arise
Who this people did despise,
Of Joseph he did nothing know,
So he them oppressed with woe.

Their sons he bid the midwives kill
But they feared to do such ill ;
So still this people multiplied
God the midwives well supplied.

Pharoah seeing they disobey'd,
Had this charge upon them laid,
That infant sons should all be drown'd
This race did too much abound.

Then the deliverer was born,
One that Israel did adorn,
His parents, both of Levi's tribe,
For his first three months did hide.

And in an ark of rushes made,
On the river left the babe,
With sister standing by to see
What the infant's fate should be.

Pharoah's daughter came down to bathe,
And this infant she did save.
The sister asked her should she find
One the child to take and mind.

To this the princess did agree,
And its mother she did see,
Promising wages her to pay,—
She the babe did take away.

Moses she said should be his name,
And when older did reclaim,
When to the palace he was sent
Well he knew his real descent.

His brethren's burdens made him groan
When they were to him made known;
He one of Egypt's sons did smite,
And from Egypt took his flight.

For Pharoah sought this man to slay,
So in Midian, hid away,
A peaceful life did Moses lead,
For he Jethro's sheep did feed.

And leading through the desert side
He to Horeb did them guide,
There he beheld a bush in flame,
Not consuming it was plain.

He turned to see the reason why
God said Moses " Here am I,"
This is my holy mercy seat,
Take thy shoes from off thy feet.

And Moses trembling, greatly feared
For the Lord's Himself appeared
Telling him he would Israel save,
No more should they work and slave

As bondmen under Egypt's laws,
He should now espouse their cause,—
To Pharoah, Israel's bitter foe,
Hasten now at once and go.

To this then Moses thus replies:
All my words he will despise,
Who am I, such a work to do,
How can I to Pharaoh sue?

But God said, I will be thy stay,
This my token thou shalt say,
My name is "I AM that I AM,"
Man and earth at once I span.

The Fathers were my children three,
Their seed you I send to free;
My presence will your footsteps lead,
Will provide for every need.

The wonders which I will perform
Egypt's king will much alarm,
At last he will them all release,
Bidding them to go forth in peace.

All deck'd with jewels rich and rare,
Borrowed from th' Egytian fair,—
Moses said, I can naught achieve
Unless they in me believe.

Take now thy rod, the Lord did say,
It shall to Israel convey
The knowledge that my strength and might
Have prepared you for the fight.

For when you cast it on the ground
It will you and them astound,
Then as a serpent with a tail
It will cause you to prevail.

Proving that I do give you aid
Satan's kingdom to invade,
Your hand shall also be a sign
That your mission is divine.

When first you draw it from your breast
Leprous white, it shall attest
To the destroying power of sin,
Desolating all within.

Then when you bring it forth again
New life shall flow through each vein,
Type of the Christian's second birth,
And a sinless life on earth.

Then if these signs shall not convince
Israel nor Egypt's prince,
Another miracle behold
My great power shall enfold.

Some water on the river pour,
On and round about the shore,
To blood the water shall be changed,
All is now for thee arranged.

How plainly this did specify
That Christ for mankind should die;
His blood and water shed for man,
Was God's own appointed plan.

Still Moses very kindly pleads,
That his work his strength exceeds,
He is not eloquent, he says,
For some help he begs and prays.

Then God in anger did command
Aaron to be his right hand,
To speak the words he did approve,
Such as Pharoah's heart may move.

But if these wonders all shall fail,
And at thee this king shall rail,
Say that his first-born God will slay
Unless Israel go away.

Jacob's descendants soon believe,
Moses and Aaron they receive
As men who from the Lord were sent,
Then to Pharoah forth they went,

Saying, Israel's God demands
Their sojourn in other lands,
To make for him a sacred feast
In the wilderness at least.

Who is the Lord I should obey?
To let Israel from me stray.
Of Israel's God I nothing know,
I will never let them go.

But this king's heart like flint became,
And he did aloud proclaim
That Israel should much more endure
This would them to him secure.

This very wicked, hardened king
Thus did tears from Israel wring,
He ten of God's great plagues did see
Before Israel he set free.

But this royal sinner it is plain,
Whose soul so much guilt did stain,
The God Jehovah never knew,
So for pardon he may sue.

Still the hardening of his heart
Is enough to make us start,
To bid us watch and guard the gate
That we may avoid his fate.

Every little tempting sin
We allow to enter in
Gives Satan in our hearts a place,
Hides from us our Father's face.

We cannot say we do not know
The great love he did bestow,
His overflowing streams of grace
Ought to satisfy our race.

Yet our murmuring day by day
Like this people by the way,
Prove that we sadly set aside
He who would us guard and guide.

And that God's grand and mighty scheme,
Man from sin to try and wean,
Has not produced the tree of life
On account of Christian strife.

If we God's garden would explore,
Drive the angels from the door,
Who with a fearful flaming sword,
This our wondrous treasure hoard,

We must, united hand in hand,
Against Satan take a stand,
And bravely meet our dreadful foe.
With one well directed blow.

The miracles that Moses wrought
Should to Egypt's king have taught
That there was One whose power divine
Would accomplish his design.

Could take away from his control
Each and every human soul
Who would Him worship and obey,
Sin and evil chase away.

But pride had so destroyed his mind
That he was both deaf and blind,
He sunk himself in depths of woe,
Ere he did his Maker know.

When Pharoah perished with his host,
Moses had good cause to boast;
It was a terrible defeat,
Moses' triumph was complete.

But to the Lord in notes of praise,
Moses' voice at once does raise,
With joy they sing as they advance,
Yes, and with their timbrels dance.

A prophetess we there behold,
Leading on the young and old;
Together they do dance and sing
Praises to their God and King.

The plagues that God did Pharoah send
Ought to make us apprehend,
That all should faithfully enquire
What it is God does require.

For Adam's sin our blood has changed,
Our whole system has deranged;
And when the Nile with blood did flow,
It did this most plainly show.

The second plague did well portray
Mankind's gradual decay;
For we would never waste away
If we walked in wisdom's way.

Then the land was filled with lice,
Such are found in haunts of vice;
Where Satan does his agents prime,
Ere he leads them on to crime.

Great swarms of flies their vision dim,
This is the effect of sin,
Which slowly o'er the senses steal,
Then the eye does firmly seal.

King Pharoah tells another lie,
So the Egyptians' cattle die;
His very dreadful stubborn will
Makes his heart rebellious still.

As Pharoah did still further try
To resist the earnest cry,
That Moses did through Aaron make,
Man and beast do both partake

Of the plague of boils and blains,
Still he Moses' prayer disdains;
He through the path of sin must steer,
It is now too late to vere.

Three curses sin did round us bind,
Upon beast, the earth, mankind;
The whole of these do now bewail,
For God sends a grievous hail.

A swarm of locusts then are sent,
Which infest each house and tent;
They ate up all the holy seed
Which this people so did need.

Then did idolatry prevail,
And light altogether fail;
For three whole days black darkness reigns,
Ere King Pharoah's power wanes.

Egyptians then began to see,
Israelites they must set free;
To save themselves from further pain,
They their favor try to gain.

And for their journey to prepare,
Send them jewels rich and rare;
Moses then, Israel did command,
To prepare to leave that land.

And God a sacrifice to pay,
Each household a lamb to slay;
But if the family be few,
One lamb will suffice for two.

No spot or blemish must defile,
Like a heart devoid of guile;
This God's most holy, sacred feast
Requires purity at least.

Then in the evening when you kill,
Its blood on the side-posts spill,
And also on the top, above,
As a token of my love.

With justice I will mercy blend,
For the cross will you defend;
When my destroying angel comes,
Dwellings marked with blood he shuns.

Begin at once, my lamb prepare,
With fire roast it, and beware
That not one fragment does remain—
Either eat or burn with flame.

With loins well girded, shoes on feet,
Staff in hand, then quickly eat;
For thus my Passover shall be
A great means of grace to thee.

For Egypt's first-born now must die,
And at midnight they will cry;
The king will then my tribes release,
For his thraldom now must cease.

What Moses said, did all take place,
That night they all left in haste;
Arise and go, were Pharoah's words,
With your cattle, flocks and herds.

Six hundred thousand forthwith went
On foot, out of Egypt sent;
Their father Joseph's bones did bare,
As they formerly did sware.

Unleavened bread they with them take,
Which they on their journey bake;
Their dough and kneading troughs they bound,
In their clothes, their shoulders round.

In pillar of a cloud by day,
The Lord led them on their way;
In a pillar of fire by night,
He dispensed to them his light.

And yet perceive they greatly fear,
When King Pharoah's host drew near;
Let us, they say, become his slaves,
Ere he sends us to our graves.

Moses alone has faith to see
They should perish in the sea;
He knew well sinners could not tread
Where he had his people led

Without the very means of grace,
Christ designed for all men's race;
The Lord he says will for you fight,
Stand and see his power and might.

Then he, who wind and seas obey
Swept the king and host away;
The Lord this people then did fear,
And his servant Moses hear.

As long as all their paths were smooth,
They with reverence did move;
But their murmurings they repeat,
When they bitter water meet.

This people then to Moses cry,
He does to the Lord apply;
A tree the Lord did to him show,
Which he was from him to throw

Into the waters, them to heal,
All their virtues to reveal;
He did so, and it made them sweet,
God's first text he did repeat.*

And when God's laws we keep from choice,
Hear and heed his still small voice;
This tree will from the waters rise,
And its fruit will make us wise.

Then should we in their Elim camp,
With this never-failing lamp;
Beneath its palms we will repose,
Free from all our present woes.

From thence, their journey they pursue,
Having Sinai in view,
And when they reach the land of sin,
Again murmurings begin

Because their bread did seem to fail,
They their leader did assail;
God's glory Israel could not see,
Though for them he dried the sea.

They worshipped at a worldly shrine,
Ever ready to repine;
Are not Christians much the same,
Daily, also, they complain.

---

* Exodus xv, 26

Manna and quails then God did rain,
This his people to sustain;
There fell each day a certain rate,
For each one an omer weight.

But on the sixth day they did find
Double portion of each kind;
That a holy, heavenly ray
Might pervade the Sabbath-day.

Our souls on that day should commune
With our God, the great Triune,
Who all his wonders will disclose
When we on him do repose.

For God does still for man produce,
All things needful for his use,
Though now scattered far and wide,
Earth does food for all provide.

But like the Israelites of old,
We our worship still withhold;
Our various idols intervene,
And God's glory from us screen.

Again this people Moses chide.
He does to his God confide,
If water he does not supply,
They will stone him till he die.

To God he lifts his heart in prayer,
Asking him his life to spare.
To Moses God at once accedes,
Hears and answers when he pleads.

The Rock of Horeb bids him smite,
With his rod he does it strike,
Fresh water then from it did flow,
Thus God's power he did show.

A type of Christ the smitten Rock,
Who, when all around did mock,
Did streams of living water yield,
Which sin hitherto has sealed.

Amalek now appears in sight,
Prepared with Israel to fight;
Moses in Joshua confides;
O'er their army he presides.

Go forth and fight, is his command,
While I stand with rod in hand,
With Hur and Aaron on the hill,
You our enemies will kill.

When Moses hands he upward held,
Joshua with sword expelled,
But when he weary let them down,
Fortune on them seem'd to frown.

So Hur and Aaron lent their aid,
And his hands they firmly staid,
This union caused them to prevail
Over him who did assail.

And when our Christian Churches three
All entwine into a tree,
Our prayers will reach Jehovah's throne,
And produce the missing stone,

Whose light will us electrify,
Men and earth quite purify;
The banner then which waves around
Will Great Amalek confound.

———

Christian Pilgrims you must now awake,
And begin at once together to rake,
Thorns, briars and weeds, now hid from our gaze,
Will soon be expos'd by God's holy ray.

A broken cistern no water can hold,
Such is the state of the Christian fold,
Its truths are all scattered here and there,
Every one claiming an equal share.

The devil has done his best to divide
The Christian Churches on every side,
But the Church of God must united be,
And from Satan's devices set quite free.

There's a hand that moves, a mysterious hand,
Who sprinkles his seed in every land,
Who chooses a humble servant, 'tis true,
To purify, alter and make things new.

That servant is ready and willing both
To suffer, work, and has plighted her troth
To spend the energies God has given
To bind the Church with the cords of Heaven.

www.ingramcontent.com/pod-product-compliance
Lightning Source LLC
Chambersburg PA
CBHW030737230426
43667CB00007B/750